WHEN LIGHT FADES AWAY HOPE REMAINS

Illuminating the Path Through Life's Dark Moments

Willy Gakunzi

10-10-10
Publishing

WHEN LIGHT FADES AWAY HOPE REMAINS:
Illuminating the Path Through Life's Dark Moments
www.whenlightfadesawayhoperemains.com
Copyright © 2023 Willy Gakunzi

Paperback ISBN: 978-1-77277-693-5
Hardcover ISBN: 978-1-77277-694-2

Publisher
10-10-10 Publishing
Markham, ON
Canada

Printed in Canada and the United States of America

Dedicated to:
God the source of true light.
Kayla and Shayna Gakunzi.
Your love and resilience are exceptional.
I am who I am today because I have you in my life.
I am proud to be your father!
Love, memories, and the light we carry.
Your impact outlives your physical existence.

Contents

Acknowledgements

I HAVE RELIED HEAVILY on others during the creation of this memoir. I would not have found courage to grab a pen and sit to document my life journey in an open and vulnerable manner, if it hadn't been for the encouragement and motivation, and a lot of grace, that was bestowed on me from all sides by friends and family. Some of you might be caught by surprise knowing that your contribution has been indescribably impactful to me. For you all, I am grateful for your constant support. I will do my best to be as elaborate in my acknowledgement as I can.

Before anyone else, I must thank **GOD**, the giver and sustainer of my life. His grace and mercies to me have been renewed every single morning. I will forever be grateful!

Second, I am grateful for my two wonderfully gorgeous daughters, **Kayla** and **Shayna,** who have been indispensable throughout the process. You have both played every role a person can play in the writing of the book: asking me what I am writing about and the reason why I am writing, reminding me to sleep on time, putting a smile on my face when the emotions were heavy, and contributing to my inspiration. It is no exaggeration to say that this book would not be the same without you being part of the process; the book might not exist at all. Thank you!

To my mother, **Nyirankamirwa,** and brothers, **Rwigemera, Mutware, Albert, Jules, Aimable, Jimmy, Thierry** and the entire

Makuza family, thank you for your support before and during the process of putting this memoir into shape. I would not have been the person I am today without my mother's prayers and unconditional family love, whether I acknowledged them or even when I just took them for granted. Thank you, family, for your resilience. My brother **Jules**, you have always been my inspiration and role model to emulate. From the stories of how life in the city looks like, which was imaginary for me at the time you told them, to your selfless sacrifice to make sure I had access to education, you have been the brother in adversities and a pillar to lean on. Papa **Sterken**, Mama **Dea,** and sister **Jacoline**, I am grateful for having been adopted into your family, which became my family. I am so grateful to God for orchestrating my life in the way he did, which led me to meeting you and becoming a family. Papa, you have stood as a father where my biological father could not, and I know he is proud of you. Sister Jaco, words would fall short if I were to talk about you. Thank you!

My deep appreciation extends to tonton **Malic** and auntie **Gertrude**; thank you for believing, loving, and supporting us all these years. You have and continue to play your parenting role to me and the girls exceptionally. Sister **Claudine**, thank you for standing with us and accepting to contribute to this memoir.

I am thankful to all my friends who have impacted and challenged me in one way or another. **Dr. Ruvebana** and **Apolline**, thank you for your brotherhood and sisterhood. Your review, your contribution to the content of the book, words of appreciation, and critical feedback were monumental to the birth of this book. **John** and **Darlene,** thank you for walking this trail called life with me for all these many years. Your constructive feedback and contribution to this memoir made it even more balanced. **Pastor Edouard** and **Irene,** thank you for the time we spent shaping each other as we navigated life together as young couples. **Gody** and **Landry,** your love and friendship is the very definition of what lifetime friendship is. My brother **Ben Tumwine,** your friendship has passed the test of time and distance. Thank you for the memories created in Groningen and after. **Dr. Semwogerere** and **Peace, Andrew** and **Barbara,** and **Mugarura and Dorcas,** thank you for being true and genuine friends for the past five years. The long and late rotational dinners, the laughs, and talks have been the strongest pillars to lean on as I navigated the grief and the process of writing this memoir. Thank you for accepting to be part of our lives. **Pastor Maombi** and **Ruphin,** you have been the cover I needed when the winter season knocked at my door. Pastor Maombi, thank you for the late night, for the cries and prayers. Your encouragement throughout the whole process has been a strong enabler that resulted in the memoir coming together. **Pamela** and **Armand,** my sister from another mother and my brother-in-law, your love and friendship have been one of the blessings I am proud of. Thank you, Pamela, for the long and real talk; thank you for challenging me to push boundaries. My dearest **Elsa** and **Olivier,** your friendship and the level of admiration leave me with a humbled appreciation. Your encouragement in this endeavor has been instrumental. To my sister **Dr. Titi,** thank you for your continued support; from day one you have been an unwavering supporter of all my initiatives. Thank you!

To my sister **Yvonne** and brother **Jared,** there are people that heaven place in our path in the right time and place. You are those people to me, and the girls. Thank you is not enough!

I am thankful for my sisters **Suzanne** and **Marion.** Thank you for your support, encouragement, and guidance in the crafting of the projects that preceded this memoir. Your continued support in expertise and heart of worship are some of the traits I will always emulate to be impactful.

This book would not be here, this year, without the encouragement and motivation from my sister **Barbara** and brother **Obed.** Barbara was the first person who asked me why I was not writing a book, and I promised her that I was going to start putting my initial draft together (I had started writing in isolation, especially the love letters as you will read below) in March. Thank you for keeping me accountable to my commitment. Brother Obed, your critical and straight to the point feedback were what I needed at the critical phase of the writing process. Thank you for daring to challenge, without a filter.

I am also grateful for my church community at **Church on the Queensway.** To my senior leader, **Pastor Billy,** your teaching of the word and your leadership is a strong pillar I have leaned on for the past 6 years I have been attending church and serving under your leadership. To **Pastor Roger,** your mentorship, your heart of service, and your wealth of knowledge when it comes to servicing the vulnerable have been a deep well to draw from. Thank you for mentoring me and supporting my initiatives. To the pastoral team, **Pastor Ed, Pastor Dawson, Pastor Arthur, Pastor Sarah, Pastor Saundra, Pastor Brandon, Pastor Ebe, and Pastor Ron,** you have all impacted my life and that of my family in many ways. Thank you for allowing God to use you to impact many.

To my worship leader, **Pastor Kibwe,** thank you for your extremely talented yet very humble heart in every aspect. Thank you for having believed in my talent as we recorded and produced the very first song I ever put out there. To the whole leadership team, sister **Vanessa,** and sister **Sulleyma,** thank you for your inspiration. To the whole team, I cannot thank you enough. You have all been the synergy that made this journey possible. Your music talent is beyond comparison.

Acknowledgements

To Apostle **Joshua Selman,** you have impacted and inspired my life through your holistic transformational teaching. Yes, you have unveiled the light that has illuminated my life. Thank you for being the powerful vessel through which many lives are being impacted!

To Apostle **Dr. Gitwaza,** thank you for your friendship, your teaching, and the contribution you made in my family's life. I will forever treasure the visit you paid us at our home, even after a very packed weekend of conference. You are a true leader!

To Apostle **Mignonne,** I am grateful and so thankful for your heart of a mother. Your call when my heart felt heavy like a stone and no one seemed to understand, will always be something I treasure in my heart. Thank you for accepting to be a vessel through which I was able to quench my thirst during that particular season. The world needs mothers like you!

To **Helen Chu,** thank you for your exceptional services and friendship. Your encouragement and guidance have helped me pick my pieces and dared to acquire property when it seemed impossible. I will always need your services.

To my work community, former and current FRR leaders, thank you for your leadership. **Claudio, Doug, Darin,** and **Jeff,** I am so grateful for the environment you create that allows me to excel in my responsibilities. A special thank you to **Erik Shaub** for your mentorship and trust bestowed upon me from day one. Your support and exemplary leadership for the past decade have been instrumental in my career. I am forever grateful. To **Paul Donaldson,** my former manager and current peer, you have taught me what leadership is. Thank you for all the contribution in my career and personal life for the past 5 years. I owe you friendship forever. I am also grateful to the whole senior leadership at Wolters Kluwer; **Nancy and**

Karen, your leadership has made my experience at Wolters Kluwer an interesting and worthwhile journey.

To my team, **Majid, Ashish, Chris, Naresh, Ganesh,** and those who have moved on to other responsibilities, working with you has constantly shaped me into a better person. Your knowledge and creativity were the engine behind my winning of the GRC CEO Award for 2021. Thank you! To my peers around the globe, thank you for all your contribution.

To my publisher, **Raymond Aaron,** thank you for making the writing experience a smooth process. Your advice and guidance have made this possible. Thank you for writing the foreword for this memoir.

Foreword

In the tapestry of human experience, there are threads woven from moments of joy and sorrow, love and loss, triumph, and defeat. Life, like a canvas, reveals itself through myriad shades of light and darkness, and it is within these interplays that your story finds its purpose. *When Light Fades Away, Hope Remains* delves deep into this intricate tapestry, inviting you to embark on a journey that explores the profound resilience of your human spirit.

In an era where uncertainty and challenges often cast their shadows, Willy's words become a beacon of light, guiding you through the labyrinthine corridors of your own emotions. This book is not just a collection of anecdotes; it's a sanctuary for the heart, a place where pain is acknowledged, hope is nurtured, and the beauty of perseverance is celebrated.

Throughout the pages of *When Light Fades Away, Hope Remains,* Willy takes you on a pilgrimage through the highs and lows of life. With each chapter, a new facet of the human experience is unveiled. The raw vulnerability with which Willy shares personal stories will be an intimate bond between the two of you. The universal themes of loss, heartache, and adversity are met with courage, wisdom, and an unwavering belief that even in the darkest of moments, a glimmer of hope remains.

Willy's narrative voice is a soothing balm for your wounded soul. With eloquent prose and a compassionate spirit, the author traverses the landscapes of grief, allowing you to not only witness the pain but also to find solace in the recognition that you are never alone in your struggles. The stories shared here are not meant to dwell solely in the realm of sorrow; rather, they kindle a flame of resilience that dances brightly against the backdrop of life's challenges.

As you turn the pages of this book, be prepared to confront your own vulnerabilities and aspirations. Allow Willy's words to wash over you, reminding you that even when faced with adversity, hope is an indomitable force that can illuminate even the darkest corners of your existence. *When Light Fades Away, Hope Remains* is an ode to your spirit's capacity to endure, to transform, and to rise above the shadows. Through these pages, Willy extends a hand, inviting you to embark on a shared journey toward healing, strength, and the unwavering belief that hope is a constant companion, guiding you through life's most challenging chapters.

In a world that often feels fragmented, this book serves as a poignant reminder that you are part of a collective story, woven together by threads of experience, emotion, and the enduring power of hope. So, as you embark on this transformative voyage, allow yourself to be captivated by the stories within and discover, as Willy has, that even in the midst of fading light, hope remains your greatest source of strength.

Raymond Aaron
New York Times Bestselling Author

"The minute I heard my first love story,
I started looking for you, not knowing how
blind that was. Lovers don't finally meet somewhere.
They're in each other all along."
~ Rumi~

Introduction

My Story

I t's around 10 p.m. and it's still sunny in the heart of the spring in the Netherlands. It has been a long day with a couple of friends, who have left their mother lands in search for a better future. The reasons behind these exoduses of brilliant young men and women can be explained by a multitude of causes. Some have fled their countries because of persecutions of all kinds, stemming from wars, domestic violence, genocides, famine, and the like. Some others have left their countries because of economic reasons and/or education. As a young person without hopes for future, the only hope is to take advantage of any opportunity that presents itself at your door as you hope to find greener pasture elsewhere.

In the year of 2003, I found myself seeking asylum in the Netherlands because of the wars that had been going on in my country of birth, the Democratic Republic of Cong (DRC), and also for economic reasons. My family had moved to Rwanda right after the 1994 genocide against the Tutsis, after the effect of that horrific and tragic event had spilled over to DRC. In the pursuit for hope, I found a way to get to Europe, the Netherlands, and claimed asylum. I will discuss more about my journey to the Netherlands that led me to meeting my light, in another chapter later on.

That evening in May 2004, I found myself with my brother and lifetime friend John in a foreigner land that I had never imagined living in. John and

I then lived in a refugee camp in the land of the White man. We decided to call our friend, Edouard, whose whereabouts we had just learned of. During our conversation, he dropped something that was to change my life for good.

As the conversation evolved, our friend Edouard told us about a very beautiful, God-fearing, and well-behaved young lady he had met, and that he would want us to meet one day. We asked him questions about that gorgeous soul, and as boys would talk, we spent a good amount of time talking just about her. At some point during our trio talk, I said that I would be interested in meeting her. The conversation heated, between boys, as both John and Edouard made fun of me. As we continued to talk about her, there was a sense of happiness in my heart that I did not really understand. To conclude that boys talk, we all jokingly concluded that if I would ever be interested, they would support me and be happy for me.

The thought of meeting the beautifully described lady stuck in my head, and the interest increased as the days passed. I had never thought of being in a love relationship up until that particular evening. As time passed, I started picturing how happy I would be to find that same person as she was described, and how happy we would be together. Two days after, I talked to Edouard on the phone, and I inquired how the beautiful one was doing. I also asked him if he could let me know the next time he was with her so that I could talk to her on his phone.

In the next few days, I finally managed to talk to the mysterious, beautiful lady on the telephone. I will reveal her name later on; just hang in there.

From that first call, as we continued to talk, my interest exponentially increased, and my conviction became firm. I was wholeheartedly convinced that she would be my wife, even though I had not yet met her nor seen her picture. This is prior to Facebook and other social media platforms where you can stalk and find out who a person is before you meet them. I relied on my friend's description and my instinct.

On June 5, 2004, I finally met the purest human being I had ever encountered. Purest because of the peace she procured for people around her. Purest because of her genuine and authentic smile. Purest because of her love and conviction she firmly held on to when it came to her faith in God. I do remember she was wearing a black shirt, brown trousers, and beige sandals. We met at a church service on a Saturday, and I was to sing while playing my acoustic guitar. Boy, I pulled my best out that day. I remember singing the song called "Above All" by Lenny LeBlanc. After the church service, we were finally able to greet and officially introduce ourselves. This was a humble beginning to a rich and yet challenging life and love story of my life.

As you journey with me through the pages of this memoire, I will share with you the light that illuminated my life—the life that death extinguished in the physical way but continues to shine throughout my life and that of our two daughters, and the lives of many that have come into contact with her. I will take you to a journey of self-discovery through love, loss, grief, and hope that makes life possible even after the death of your other half.

I will attempt and strive to share my hopes through these life events, which we all undergo in many shapes and forms and at various stages of our life. I also promise you to be vulnerable while sharing what I think is important; otherwise, if I would write every account, this memoire would become a series of many books.

I have discovered the light in me that was lit as my path crossed the path of my princess and redefined my life in its entirety. I did not know that love could be so pure and yet be cut short at the climax of life. I did not know that you could love and be loved so much, and yet find the courage to live after death has taken away half of your heart. I did not know that love is more powerful than death itself, to the point that it unveils the myriads of possibilities life can offer amidst grief and loss. When this experience is well understood and lived, it can give life to life itself.

Let me thank you in advance for allowing me to talk to you through the pages of this book. It is a privilege and honor to have your attention shared with me as I share my life story with you; rest assured that I do not take this for granted. I will, as I promised already, try my best to share my journey with you in the most open and vulnerable way possible. I would be delighted to continue to have a conversation with you even after we have talked through these pages. Hang in there; I need you to stick around as we both navigate through my light.

Let's go.

Genesis

Why I Chose to Write This Memoir

I am lost. I am in complete darkness. I have just heard the news that my light had been rushed into the hospital in a paramedic ambulance car. Little did I know that five hours after that call I received on that Thursday, at 3:53 p.m., on November 8, 2018, I was about to go through excruciating pain and agonizing hours that I would never wish anyone to experience.

My mind is frozen, I am numbed, and I haven't realized that my life is to be altered in a way that I did not think. I was not prepared to go through what was happening.

I am on a freeway, driving from North York, a neighborhood north of Toronto, and I am driving south to downtown Toronto. I am listening to a song called "You Made a Way," by Travis Greene. I hear a voice calling from the back seat of my car—but I am by myself in the car. The voice asked me a strange question, with multiple sub questions: What if today is the last day you will see your wife alive? What will you say and how will you behave? How about the dreams and the plans you have, yours and hers combined? Will you allow them to be silenced with her?

I entered into a conversation with the voice, without a physical person talking to me, and my answer was very clear and with confidence: I will be strong for her and for our little princesses. I will boldly pay tribute to her.

I started playing out in my mind what I would say as my farewell speech as I drove (I will share that speech later in the following chapters). I continued to answer those questions and finally said, "I will not allow my dreams and our dreams to be silenced with her."

This conversation happened as though I was watching a live movie on the screen. It felt surreal but, at the same time, I was calm and peaceful. I did not think or realize that it was an actual preparation and rehearsal of what was about to happen in real life. I continued my drive as I listened to the same music that was on repeat: "You made a way when our backs were against the wall, and it looked as if it was over; you made a way." This song, without realizing it, was to become my life story and testimony in the hours, days, weeks, months, and years that followed till today.

I continued my ride through rush hour traffic, not fully comprehending what was happening. Since that day, I made an unequivocal decision that, as long as I still have life in me, I will empty myself with all the riches and potential that the creator has endowed with me. I will empty myself through achieving and accomplishing the plans and dreams I shared with my light, as I do not believe in hazardous life encounters.

This book is one way to empty myself and share my light and dreams with you in the hope that you will gain value and strive to live a life that is result-driven, a life with a purpose. As I write these pages, it has been 4 years, coming to five years in a few months, since the light of my life was physically dimmed and her voice silenced, but as I promised in my conversation with the invisible interlocutor, the light continues to shine and illuminate my world through memories and work we do.

This book is one of the many initiatives I have undertaken in the journey of emptying myself before I join the myriads of those who have gone ahead of us. It is also a testament of hope we have that comes from the true light that transforms our lives and empowers us to live with hope and peace, even when life denies us the right to do so. I encourage you to find ways and means to not leave this part of eternity with books, songs, businesses, projects, etc. unfinished. And I hope and pray that everything you were endowed with will serve the humanity in your lifetime, and through those you will have illuminated in the course of your life journey.

Stay with me!

PART ONE

JOURNEY TO MY LIGHT

"I'm a simple man. Grew up in a small town.
Came from humble beginnings. No silver spoon."
~ Robin S. Sharma ~

Chapter 1

Humble Beginnings

Thank you for staying with me this far. It's just the beginning of a journey that, through the next pages of this memoir, will take you through my love, losses, grief, and healing and self-discovery. I am humbled and excited that we will have an honest and deep conversation, and hopefully get our lights rekindled to shine for many lives to hope again.

You might be wondering how the story of meeting my light started in the Netherlands and in a refugee camp. How did she and I end up in that situation? This chapter will give you a glimpse of my early years that will shed light on how I found myself in the Netherlands. I believe our lives are orchestrated by and through life events that, in many cases, we do not have control over. Without knowing it, these events usher us into the next chapters of our lives.

Villager at Core

I was born in Zaire, currently the Democratic Republic of Congo. The area where I was born was, and still is to some extent, a remote area away from the civilized world, and it is virgin land with greenery, nature, rich biodiversity, and people that live a very modest, authentic, and primitive lifestyle, at least they did until early 2000.

When I was growing up, in the 80s, my life could be summarized as a very positive and trouble-free life. My childhood wearies I can recall were when calves went missing when we got distracted by our village boys' games, running off hills, swimming in the rivers, and playing football (soccer). As a young man in my culture, my primary duty, before and after school hours, was to look after calves, to make sure they were taken to get water, slept under shade and were returned in the compound around sunset, before their mothers returned from grazing.

I did not worry about watching TV or playing video games, simply because this was unknown to me. My gadget was playing football (soccer) barefooted, swimming in rivers, climbing trees for nature and wild fruits, and herding my family's herds. These were my activities until I reached the age to go to school, which was between 6 and 7 years.

There was a measuring stick for knowing that you were ready to go to school. As long as you could not touch your other ear by stretching your arm across your head, you were deemed too young to go to school. The day you could touch your other ear, that was the day you were school aged. I wonder if some kids went to school early and others late, depending on their height. With fading memory, I do remember going to school the first year, but then I wasn't, and I was not sure what the reason was. It might have been the case that when I got to school, the teacher tested me using that measuring stick and decided that I was still too young to attend school. This was good news for a boy at that time as it meant more time to play in nature without an adult's control. The next year, I did return and started school, and if I remember correctly, it was in 1987 that I started primary 1.

Yes, primary 1; not kindergarten. I did not go to daycare or kindergarten. These are concepts that did not exist, and they still do not exist in my mother high land of Mulenge in the Democratic Republic of

Congo. I will cover my study journey in more detail in later chapters. However, for the sake of this early introductory discussion, the years that followed were full of mixed emotions. I still do not understand how I amounted to something, when I look back at how the education system was. Imagine that my first exposure to running water, electricity and power, books and other education material, was only when I was in secondary school. Hang in there; I will cover that in more detail. With this in mind, I can only say that life's current circumstances are in no way to be used as prediction of what the life of an individual will be tomorrow. We oftentimes judge people's futures based on the wrong references—today's circumstances—which might lead to acting in the wrong way towards those we perceive through today's lenses. I have come to discover that the achievements admired today are in no way to be compared with the ones we have not yet seen. Because of this, I have learned to honor everyone that crosses my path.

Family

I do not have many memories of my early childhood life, such as pictures and video images, other than the wonderful, faded memory of a life that was natural and trouble free. I was born in a family of 10 siblings. Just imagine how that home might have been for my parents. My parents had given life to 9 boys and 1 girl. The first 4 were boys and then a girl, and 5 more boys. I was born number 9.

Being among the youngest in the family, there is much that I did not get to experience. The fifth born, who was the only girl, I was told, passed on when she was around 1 year old. And my brother that came before me, also did not make it to toddler age. I also do not remember living with my elder brothers under the same roof. By the time I could make sense of life, my 3 elder brothers had already been married. In fact, their wives were my babysitters! I remember growing up with my young brother and the 6th in the birthline. The 7th in birth was at my grandma's home. I barely remember him living with us at home.

Another memory that I did not have the chance to build is with my father. My father, Pastor Philip Makuza, passed on when I was only 2 years old. I do not remember how it was to be in a home with both parents. I was told that we were very close; to the point that in the days that followed his passing, I would not allow anyone to sit on his chair in the church. Apparently, I was determined and strongly believed that my dad was coming back. As I grew—I was told this story—I would stay outside and look up to the sky, waiting to see my father coming back. On multiple occasions, I would run to the house whenever I heard the sound of an airplane in the sky, and I would scream, hoping that the pilot would fly low enough to take me with them up to the sky to meet and bring my papa back.

Despite these non-existent childhood memories, I was raised in a very loving and coherent family, with a very strong and strict mother that taught us true love and made sure that we would live lives she and our father did not have the opportunity to live. The love that I experienced as a child—I would disclaim with a high level of confidence that this was the norm in our culture and environment—was not necessarily verbal. I do not remember my mother or siblings telling me that they love me. I do not remember saying it back. However, the love was lived. We did not have much in terms of material possessions; nevertheless, we had each other. We had a natural and integral society that made our lives as children sweet and worriless. I am pretty sure our elders did know more than we did.

We lived a life, as children, without any pressure from the outside. We were not exposed to what was happening elsewhere outside our village's perimeters, which allowed us to sustain a high level of community love, despite the modest lifestyle.

Pure Community

Our main source of nutrients in my community/society was milk and vegetables, including beans, maize, and potatoes that were homegrown. Mothers would grind maize to make flour that was used to make ugali (a dish made from corn flour, cassava flour or wheat flour), which we ate with vegetables and/or bean sauce. I must say that children were mainly milk fed—we would just drink fresh milk from the cow, morning and evening.

We lived in huts made of bamboo, mud, and grass as construction materials. These modest houses were both our kitchens and, to some extent, our living rooms. However, when growing up, because my father was a noble, he did have two houses—one for a kitchen and which also served as a bedroom for some kids, and a second home that was our living home. The second home was the parent's and young children's main home. These houses were not locked, nor were they built of durable materials; however, there were no stories of thefts or break-ins. Communities lived in perfect harmony, and neighbors were each other's watchmen. Children would play outside and eat at whatever house the eating time found them in.

I also remember my mother making ugali and sending me to neighbors to bring sauce to eat with it. This was a common practice. Every day, we had kids coming for either this or that. You did not have to starve because you had a shortage of one recipe, and you did not even have to think twice before you started making supper. Mothers would prepare meals with what they had in the house and then send kids for whatever was missing.

This was the same for milk. No home should be deprived of milk, whether they had a milking cow or not; the whole village had to have a good supply of milk. In many circumstances, families borrowed milking cows from other families until they could produce their own milk. There were poor people who did not have cows of their own; however, everyone was supplied with milk. In my culture, milk and cows are the core of our health and riches. In fact, till now, our riches are measured in terms of cows. The more you have, the richer you are.

My community childhood memory is that of peace—violence free, theft free, and plenty of unspoken love and harmony.

Fatherless

It was 1981, during the wedding ceremony of Rwigemera, my elder brother and the first born to our parents. My father stood to give his speech and revealed his 30-plus-years secret covenant he had made with his creator. That day, he publicly narrated that he was ready to finish his journey on Earth. He had made a promise to God that when his first son married, he would pass on the baton as a symbol that he was ready to join the cloud of many who had transitioned. After this powerful and emotional speech, he handed over his Bible to his son. He concluded his speech by saying: "I don't know how many years I still have to live, and I don't know if God is still wanting me to go home right way. But what I had promised has come to pass. I am ready to go home, today, or whenever God will call me home."

In the year that followed, my mother said Papa spent it sleeping on the ground, praying for Mum and his sons. He would tell Mum that he was going home and that he would want her to be strong and stay where we lived. Because my father was an ordained pastor of the church, he insisted to his wife that she should stay at church, as if he knew he was transitioning. On November 30, 1982, my father took his last breath and went to be with his creator. One day before he passed, he called all the church leaders in the Minembwe area—this is like a whole district—and they all gathered around him and said their goodbyes. He was not sick; his time to go home had arrived.

On the night Dad passed on, he was with my mum and his cousin and brother. He asked them to help him lie down, and he said that there were two men that had come to take him home. He gave his soul and rested eternally. Keep this occurrence in mind; we will see a similar occurrence later on.

Growing up without a father figure was hard and confusing, as I did not understand why other kids had fathers while my siblings and I did not. But because of my society and culture, and the time and environment we lived in, I did not know of any other ways of communicating and explaining these life dilemmas. I lived with this question and a loss I did not get a chance to grieve. This ungrieved loss created an extreme love and appreciation for my mother, but I did not know how to express it. I, therefore, developed a sense of responsibility at a very early age. As soon as I could make sense of life, I resolved to help my mother with whatever I could.

I mentioned earlier that many boys' activities were centered around cows and their calves. However, I found myself doing activities and duties that were predominantly done by our sisters. That included collecting firewood, fetching water, and grinding maize to produce flour. I also started cleaning the house compound with my sisters-in-law when I was a young boy. I came to find out later how these early experiences prepared me for a life I would live later (more about that in later chapters).

With this life experience, I missed my dad without even knowing that I did. I did not have his memory, and I also wasn't told or taught how to navigate life without a father. I remember later on blaming my elder brothers for not playing a fatherly role, but I came to realize that they did go through harder times than I did, because our dad passed when they had started making tough life decisions and they needed him even more than I did (for lack of a better description). Boy, life became hard without our dad, who was also a noble and strong pillar in our community at large.

My father was among the earlier converts to Christianity. These were men and women in some cases that got exposed to the outside civilizations. My dad was taught to read by a supernatural miracle (I will not dwell on this; it's a book topic by itself), and he later met with Christian missionaries that gave him a Bible and song books that formalized his education level. This is an experience that many men and women in the late 1940s and early 1950s went through in the high plateau of Mulenge. There was a wind of revival in that area, and those who experienced it were later trained and became the pioneers of the education system that allowed the next generation to access the external world.

This noble, young father of a large family, and a leader in society, was gone. He was gone when he was only 42 years old. His departure left a very big vacuum in our family, to the point that my 3 elder brothers completed their secondary education with difficulties. But because of his legacy, somehow, doors were opened, and we all managed to get secondary education. I was the first to get a master's degree. There is a Bible reference that says that the offspring of a righteous man will not be forgotten in the land of the living. I can testify that this has surely been proven true in my family life. All odds were against us after our father left us. How could a village girl, without any education, raise 8 boys and send them to school while facing the then cultural challenges? I am amazed by how God finds a way to make his promises come to pass, even when they have been seemingly cut short.

As I write this section, all 8 brothers are alive with their families. My mother has grandchildren and great-grandchildren. Makuza lives through them all. Truly, when the light we carry is fully grasped to the point that we live our lives according to it, this very light will benefit many generations.

My Education Journey

As I mentioned above, I grew up in a remote area with near zero exposure to the other parts of the country and the rest of the world. As remote as this area was, and its inhabitants particularly all being farmers and breeders, because of a high level of Christianity penetration, parents who did have a chance to access education had brought schools. From the mid-1950s, schools were built, and families started allowing their children to attend them and gain education, and by the early 1970s, there were university graduates from the area.

My father, being among the nobles in the area with access to the external world, made sure that all brothers accessed education. In fact, he was among the pioneers of the elementary school of Kakenge, the area in which I was born, where all my siblings and I started our education journey. By the time he passed on in the fall of 1982, all my siblings, except me and my younger brother, were in school; the four elders were all in high school.

His departure cut short the plans and the dreams he had for his boys. The first born had already left home to pursue his education in the nearest city, the city of Baraka. And the second and the third born were also scheduled to leave the next year for Bukavu, to continue their education there. Their education journey was altered as the family had to readjust to survive the loss.

My time came when I could join school. I was excited because my agemates were also attending school. At the same time, it was a disruption of my free time to play in nature. I do not have many memories of my early school experience, but a few things stuck in my memory.

I remember that we all had to wear school uniforms, in blue and white. We had to wake up very early to do the morning chores, including milking cows and cleaning the calves' mangers, and then we walked for a few minutes to school. I was fortunate because the school was in our village. I know that many kids had to walk a few kilometers to get to school.

As soon as we got to school, we would be playing football (soccer), touch, and doing lots of running. Once the bell rang, we all had to line up by class level in the school court. Then we would sing the Zaire national anthem. We would put our right thumbs on the left side of our chests, right on top of the heart, as a symbol of royalty to the Zaire ruling party and the president. It was prohibited to make any move when we were singing the national anthem. After the national anthem, we would sing our allegiance to the ruling party. The song had a line that went as follows: "It is a big lie for those who think that the ruling party will have an end; it is a lie." Facts are stubborn; everything does have an end.

Another memory that stayed with me till today, was the level of strictness of teachers. As students, we were encouraged to ask challenging questions to teachers. When it came to punishment, it was rather strict and extreme, involving slaps and kneeling for a considerable amount of time. Even though this might sound less than pleasant, the experience did build positive traits in me (I do know that it is the case for my classmates). We learned to respect elders, and especially to not talk when an elderly person is addressing you. We learned to focus and pay attention when we were assigned tasks to work on.

Long story short, despite these difficult conditions we were in, we studied and enjoyed it. I was not the smartest kid in class; however, I did well. I never repeated any class, and I was always in the first 10 in class, and most of the time in the first 5. From grade 9, we started studying science and electronics, like the notion of movement, but we had not even seen a bike. We had seen cars that brought military personnel and priests to the nearby Catholic parish, but I had personally never boarded a car. So, throughout elementary and middle school, our education was theoretical in nature—no experience; not even being exposed to the material we learned. I still remember stories that my brother, Jules, who had gone for his education in Bukavu and then continued to Lubumbashi for university, would narrate for us. Whenever he would come back to the village for vacations, he would tell us how things are done in the cities, and it all seemed like fiction in my mind.

My first exposure to labs and experimental education was in 1994 when we moved to Rwanda after the genocide against the Tutsi. Although the country had almost been completely destroyed, the little that remained was my very first encounter with modern education and a modern lifestyle at large. I joined one of the best schools at that time in the country: Groupe Scolaire Officiel de Butare (Astrida). It is a very renowned school that educated the first elites in the African Great Lakes region.

Surprisingly, I was not behind as compared to my classmates, who had also come from different parts of Africa, and those who were in Rwanda before 1994. I continued to perform well at school and graduated my high school with a scholarship to attend the National University of Rwanda, in the faculty of science. I later on continued my university education in the Netherlands (to be revisited in the chapters below).

Stateless Community

Although I grew up in what I call pure community fabric, in the years that I started making sense of life, things had changed drastically. I heard stories of people who were being imprisoned for no reason; cows and other possessions were being taken from the population by the military, and there was discrimination that my community was victim of because we are Tutsi. I was very young, but I do remember that in 1990, things were not as they used to be. My community was publicly discriminated against. Consequently, young people from my village started joining the struggle that was ongoing to liberate Rwanda; at the same time, discrimination increased. I also remember that elderly people were saddened by what was happening in Rwanda as they followed the news, and they were also very concerned by the increased discrimination and threat of the genocide that was spilling over to our region.

The memories I have of law enforcement forces, military, and police personnel in Zaire (now Democratic Republic of Congo) is that they were terrifying people. Whenever they showed up, someone would either be taken away or belongings were looted and taken away. Adults would run away for safety if time allowed, and children were to stay home, hoping that nothing would happen to them. I really did not understand why the people who were in charge of our security and making sure everyone is treated equitably, were the same people who would violate the basic human rights. I recall a few events that I witnessed before I became a teenager.

Burned with a Match

The first traumatizing event I personally experienced in Zaire was when I was about 10 years old or so. It was late in the night; it must have been past midnight, and my mother, younger brother, and our sister-in-law were in our home sleeping. The next thing I remember hearing was a noise in the house; people were shouting in Lingala and Swahili. It was so terrifying that I woke up from my sleep shaking even though I did not know what was going on. It must have been going on for some time. It had been a long day at school and playing on the playground, running with friends in nature, and I was definitely in a deep sleep. I remember opening my eyes, but I could not see anything as their bright torch was right in my face. I do not remember what was being said because I was too young to even relate. They broke things in the house and took whatever they could, including kitchen utensils and food. Till today, I have not understood why that happened or what they were looking for. I never asked my mother, and I don't even think she understood what was going on that night.

After they had taken everything they could collect in the house, they lit a match and put it on my eyebrows. They made sure to leave a mark on my face. I am not sure if they wanted to burn the house or if they just wanted to hurt that little boy because they did not find any adult man in the house. I still have the scar from that burn. Next time you see me, just come close; you will see it. I will not tell which eye it is, but I trust you can closely observe, and you will see it.

I do not remember where my elder brothers had gone as I do not recall that they were home that night. Now that I think about it, they must have known about these terrifying security forces passing by and had gone hiding that night, which would explain why my sister-in-law was sleeping with us that night. It had become a common practice where village watchmen would announce the news, and all men, especially young men, would hide before the military group would reach the village.

The pure community I had grown up in was in turmoil, caused by the very people that were supposed to protect it. People started developing behaviors that were otherwise uncommon in our culture, such as plotting against neighbors to get money, stealing, and even falsifying reasons to get others into trouble, including imprisonment.

Taken Hostage for Hours

The second event I remember, which did not make sense until later, was on a sunny, late afternoon after school. It was common in our culture that after school, boys would either go to look after calves or join the elders, their fathers, brothers, or uncles, where the cows would go grazing. That afternoon, I went with my uncle to look after our village herd. Our village was basically made up of my extended family: grandparents, uncles, and their families and my family. It was around 5 kilometers from the village, and my uncle and I were about to head home. We were behind the herd as they followed their leader. This would either be a new mother cow that was in a hurry to go home, or a bull that would lead and the rest of the herd would follow. This was one of the best feelings in our breeding lifestyle: The sun sets and you are behind a herd of traditional cows with long horns, singing for them and having them respond. How I miss that!

Suddenly, we saw a group of soldiers with loads of luggage, full of all kinds of things. They were coming from the opposite direction as we headed home. We did not have the opportunity to hide or run because they were so close, and had we attempted, they would not have hesitated to send bullets our way or towards our cows. So, my uncle took my hand and assured me that nothing would happen to us. Somehow, him being with me helped. Although things had gone wrong, at that time in the early 1990s, there was still some respect for children's rights. They forced us to carry their loads to a destination we did not know.

They gave me a live chicken to carry, and we walked for the next five hours or so until we arrived at a place called Murusuku. This was the next village after crossing the Mitumba Mountains; this is a large mountainous and dense forest area that culminates to the equatorial forest in the eastern part of DR Congo. We left the place they took us from, around 3 p.m., and we arrived at that village maybe around 7 p.m. We had not eaten anything, and we were carrying loads. I, being a boy of 12 years, was carrying a live chicken they had taken, probably from one of the villages they had passed.

The lieutenant that was leading the group instructed that they should let us return, as the people in that village were to continue with them. He did give us bananas to eat on our way back. My uncle and I and another man that they had brought from a neighboring village set off for another walk back home. It was dark, in a dense and tropical forest, but we had to return. There was no other option. Additionally, back home, no one could have known what had happened to us (even though they might have suspected that we were taken by the so-called military). We arrived home late in the night, and I remember finding my mother so worried. She had not slept, not knowing her son's whereabouts. I believe that the journey back home took longer as my uncle and the other man had to carry me through the Mitumba Mountains.

Guess what? The whole herd had returned home, well and safe. But the whole village and the entire family was terrified and were waiting for us to return home.

God is my shepherd, and I shall not want. In the dark night, through thick and thin, he leads me beside still waters (Psalms 23). I still fail to understand what the land of honey and milk had become. I still fail to understand why this country that my forefathers fought for and are resting in still hates my community. Since this is about my personal account, I will not dwell on the societal aspect, lest I write another book within one!

Visiting Rwanda Is a Crime!

This event is the highlight of how wrong the country Zaire had gone in hostility against the Tutsi people in the country. Any mention of any relationship with Rwanda, in any shape or form, had become a high ticket for a lawsuit. When this event took place in the summer of 1994, it was the trigger to my journey that would eventually lead me to the Netherlands, where I was to meet "my light."

It was late summer (I should say dry season because, in Central Africa, we only have dry and rainy seasons, as all other tropical areas); I believe in August or so. It was 1994, after the genocide against the Tutsis in Rwanda. I was 13 years old, turning 14, and was now starting to make sense of things I had experienced, including the two events aforementioned, but I am still not clear on why.

As the tragic events were happening in Rwanda, we received a few people who had escaped the genocide. I would hear news on the radio about what was happening, and I did see my brothers and elders worried, but I did not know much. I also knew a few young adults who had left Mulenge to join the Rwanda liberation movement that would, fortunately, put an end to the killings of innocent Tutsis in Rwanda. One of my brothers, who was at that time working in Burundi, had also joined the movement as a cadre—cadres were the forces behind the mobilization of forces and funds to support the liberation movement. I did not know he had joined until later when we moved to Rwanda. As the situation in Rwanda deteriorated for Tutsis in the country, the hostility against the Tutsis in Zaire exponentially increased. The number of arbitrary arrests increased, which fueled the interest and incentives for young adults to flee and join the struggle, siding with the Rwanda liberation movement that would stop the genocide.

One of those heroes is the late General Byicaza Barabona. Byicaza was like a brother to me because his father, Pastor Barabona, and my father were both pastors of our home church, and both families were as close as relatives. May his soul continue to rest in peace. After liberating Rwanda, he later went back to liberate Zaire in 1996 as the genocide was now targeting my people, the Tutsi in Zaire. He unfortunately lost his life at the battle front in 2001.

Rwanda was liberated on July 4, 1994, right after many people from Mulenge were migrating to Rwanda. My eldest brother, the first born, also went to find out how the situation was and whether it was time for us to move. Upon his return, the situation in Zaire had worsened. The corrupt regime of Mobutu was now tracking everyone who had a family member who had crossed the border into Rwanda. Unfortunately, many people with malintent used the opportunity to whistle blow in exchange for money. The weeds had grown within the green vegetation where my community used to be. We did not know who had been corrupt!

Someone had signaled that my brother had just arrived from Rwanda, as if going to Rwanda was a crime at that time, and it is still the case to date, unfortunately. I do not know how my brother learned about it, so he would not sleep in his house. It was a Saturday, early morning, and a whole legion came to our village and surrounded his house. Now, my brother was sleeping with me and my younger brother in our home. I do not recall where Mum had traveled to—I believe she had already traveled to Rwanda with my two other brothers. My brother, Rwigemera, who was being hunted, told me to wake up and go to my other brother, the second in line, Pastor Mutware, and tell him to wake up and talk to those military people. At the same time, Rwigemera also woke up and went to hide in the nearest bush—we were living near a mini forest that served as a farm for vegetables, and there was a river where we would fetch water.

I went outside, shaking and not fully knowing what was going on. It was around 5 a.m., and even though the sun was coming up, it was still dark. The FAZ (Zaire Armed Force) soldiers were there, armed to their teeth in front of me. When they saw me, they called out in Lingala, which I did not understand, and then they switched to Swahili. They inquired why I was up and where I was going. In a shaky voice, I said that I was going to wake up my brother, Pastor Mutware, who wanted me to distribute church invitations to the next village. I do not know where that response came from. I wondered if this was what the Bible refers to when it talks about not being afraid of what to say when we're in difficult situations—the holy spirit will give you the right words at the right time! You might call it a lie, but I believe it was a revelation that spared my life and that of my family. A few of them followed me as I knocked at his door. I signaled in my mother tongue that there were military with me. He asked me to remain calm and assured me that he was coming out.

I remember he had a portrait of King Rwagasore of Burundi, President Kagame of Rwanda, who was leading the liberation movement in Rwanda, and late general Rwigema, who started the liberation movement of Rwanda, in his living room. Before he opened the door, he made sure that those portraits were hidden, as they would make the case worse. Seeing portraits of those individuals at that time in Zaire was a ticket to life in prison or even death. Why? I think that would be a whole book in itself.

As he came out, he announced himself as a pastor and asked what he could do for them. They were shouting and asked where his older brother was. He calmly told them that he had taken his wife to the hospital, which was not wrong. Rwigemera's wife had been sick, and he was with her, but that day he had returned home. He then signaled me to go and wake our uncle, who was a retired military man. I slipped through them and went to my uncle's house. In a few minutes, he was there, talking to the men in Lingala, and he actually rebuked them, saying that what they were doing was violating our basic human rights. The discussion became intense between the former military man and those who had come to abuse us, and in the next few minutes, I saw one military man holding a gun against my uncle's forehead. I was so terrified, but I stood there.

My uncle told him that they would do nothing to his family and our cows as long as he was there and breathing. I guess this brutal military wanted to scare him or actually shoot him, but my uncle stood firm as a real soldier who had learned the military ethics and had served his country faithfully until he retired. In the next seconds that followed, I heard shooting, and luckily the shootings were directed in the air. They shot 14 bullets and the whole village was awake; people were running in all directions. My uncle and another relative, who was visiting and had spent the night in my brother's house, were handcuffed. They were severely beaten, imprisoned for 10 days or so, and the family had to pay ransom to release them.

What had they done? Nothing but being who God created them to be. Being a Tutsi was not welcomed anymore, but having been in Rwanda was a crime that the regime hunted everyone for.

Journey Home

This was it. My family decided to move to Rwanda. The situation was extremely bad in Zaire. The people who had committed genocide in Rwanda were now planning together with the Mobutu regime to continue the same killings to eliminate Tutsi people in Zaire. Rwanda was the new and safe home for us; it was time to move. My brother, Jules, who was working in Burundi at that time and had survived the 1993 massacre in Burundi, had already crossed over to Rwanda. This was the new land of hope for people like us in the Great Lakes Region of Africa, especially those in Zaire. Mobutu and his regime had welcomed the whole army that had committed genocide in Rwanda, and together with the extremists in Zaire, they were then planning to erase the Banyamulenge (my tribe; Tutsi's living in South-Kivu province in Zaire) and all other Tutsi in Zaire.

As soon as Rwanda was liberated and the genocide was stopped by the Rwanda Patriotic Front, a mass migration from across the globe started taking place. Many families from Mulenge were moving to Rwanda to find a new home and help rebuild the country that had seen its people and infrastructure completely erased. We did not have contact with Jules, who had already crossed from Burundi, but all odds indicated he must have moved as Burundi had become less stable as well.

Coincidently, my mother had fallen sick for some time, and they could not find what she was suffering from. I was young but I do remember that she was in so much pain that she spent so many sleepless nights. A family meeting was called, and all my brothers decided that my mother and two of my other brothers should go to Rwanda for treatment, and maybe find out if it was time for the whole family to move. Because they expected Jules to have already crossed over to Kigali, it was the best option to take. The next few days, Albert, Jimmy, and my mother took off on a three-day walking trip to get to Uvira, where they would take a bus towards the border of Rwanda, in Kamanyola.

We did not hear from them for a few months as there was no means of communication available. After the genocide in Rwanda, families that survived, as well as those who had moved to Rwanda, would broadcast radio announcements to invite their family members to join. Since my mother and my three brothers had already arrived in Kigali, we would listen to the radio in the hope of hearing an announcement from Jules to join them. Months passed and the situation in Zaire continued to worsen. The day came when the announcement was aired on the radio; Jules was calling us to come to Kigali. We packed very minimal belongings and traveled for three days, walking to Uvira.

This was my first exposure to the external world—external because, in my 14th year, I had never seen electricity; I had never seen a television, or any type of city life in general. When we arrived at Uvira, looking across Tanganyika Lake in the city of Bujumbura at night was surreal. I did not understand how all houses had light at night, and life seemed to be running so fast. There were so many first experiences that I will not share here in this memoire; however, it was simply revealing and very strange to a 14-year-old boy.

Early in the morning, before the sun rose, we boarded a minibus to Kamanyola, where we would cross over to Rwanda. My brother had to pay a lot of money for a military vehicle to accompany us, as there were so many roadblocks along the highway from Uvira to the border. Fast-forward, upon arrival at the border, we were once again abused (but this time it was the last time) when the border control literally took everything we had on us—money, books, and even clothes. Because we had paid the military officer, we were let go but empty handed.

Since I left my native village in Zaire, which later become Democratic Republic of Congo, I have not had the opportunity to return.

Human in Military Uniform

The snare was broken, and we escaped. As we walked through the neutral zone towards Rwanda, the atmosphere changed. A few meters ahead of us, there were people from different governmental organizations that welcomed us with water to refresh us. They rushed us into big tents that had been installed along the highway; they fed us and we were immediately registered.

What surprised me most was the military personnel that were involved in welcoming us. These young, skinny and tall men in military uniforms hugged us genuinely and spoke my language. It was the first time seeing someone in a military uniform hugging a civilian, genuinely, and speaking in my language. They were actually people like us and it felt so different; it procured peace that I could not explain. Just a few minutes back, we were not sure that we would survive, as the Zaire military force brutalized us before letting us cross over. At the age of 14, I had experienced two opposite military dynamics, one being unreasonably violent and scary, and the other being warm, gentle, and strangely human. It felt strangely good to see military people, on their guard but welcoming and hugging civilians. Contrary to what had just happened on the other side of the border, they did not take anything from us; they did not interrogate us as though we were criminals. Rather, they hugged us, fed us, and made sure we felt safe. This was my very first good experience with this new country that had been destroyed and had lost over a million people in 100 days.

Land of Hope in the Middle of Ashes

When Rwanda was liberated, we all chanted the songs of victory and were genuinely happy that there was a place we could go and call home. I was young, but somehow I did know that Rwanda had become better than Zaire for me and my people. I knew many families that had moved, and my mother and brothers were already in Kigali.

We would listen to Radio Rwanda every day to hear the news of hope and praise of those who liberated the country, and how they invited all Rwandans to return home.

When our turn came, although I did not know what to expect, I was extremely happy, mainly because I had missed my mother so much. I just wanted to go where she was and did not care much about the place. I also did not really know the magnitude of what had just happened in that small country with people who resemble me and speak the same language as me.

From the moment we crossed the border, everything changed. Yes, the country was completely destroyed; many survivors were still under unexplainable pain and trauma, and the thickness of death was still felt in the atmosphere. Yet, at the same time, there was a light that shone through the thick darkness. Those who were coming from outside, and the survivors, joined hands and started filling the gaps. I remember that my brother, who was then a student at the National University of Rwanda, was also serving to reestablish the judicial system.

Life was still hard; supplies were limited, and the remains of war and genocide were still felt in all corners of the country. The military and law enforcement were so different from what I was accustomed to on the other side of the border, but this time they were the people to go to for help.

They walked around day and night calmly, just making sure that everyone else was at peace. This made the emptiness and the ashes of the war somehow lighter and bearable, especially for those who had experienced the tragic event. Everything was still so vulnerable and somehow unsecure. I remember one night that I was chased by a herd of dogs barking at me. These domestic animals had seen the unspeakable and had become human hunters, to say the least.

The welcoming face of resilient young men, who had just liberated the country, covered the thick and dark atmosphere after the genocide that had taken over a million innocent lives. Despair was felt all around. At the same time, the joy of life and the hope that the new leadership inspired made the shadow of death bearable. People were lost, confused, and yet hopeful. The light had dawned after a long night that lasted for 100 days. Those who survived were relieved and, at the same time, lost. After all, how do you pick up ashes and live again? Those who were returning to Rwanda after decades in exile were celebrating to finally have a country that they could call home; at the same time, they felt lost when finding a torn apart social fabric. Where would they start to rebuild the country they so hoped to live in again?

All indicators—social, economic, and even spiritual—classified life in Rwanda as nonexistent at that point in time. But there was hope that stemmed from the resilience of the Liberation Army and its leadership; there were dreams that had not been silenced, and anyone who found themselves in Rwanda strived for life.

My Becoming

My growing up and becoming a man, my exposure to life and my dream for a hopeful future, was born the day we moved to Rwanda. For the first time, I felt a sense of belonging. My years lived in Rwanda were the years that defined the man I would become later on in life.

I discovered the joy of living when we were living in Rwanda, largely because my teenage and adolescent years were lived in Rwanda, but also because I felt at home, and I was indeed home. For the first time, I did not feel strange among those I was with. For the first time, I did not have to fear that I might meet brutal and terrifying military personnel. For the first time, as I was growing, I discovered the joy of life through trial and error as a young man. I had my first crushes on young ladies; I felt love, and I was loved. It was also in Rwanda that I made the mature and conscious decision to give my life to my Savior, and I started my Christian walk and personal relationship with Jesus Christ. Briefly, my years of formation and becoming were lived in Rwanda.

If you stay with me, this book will take you through my journey to finding my light, and the hope that remains despite the setback. The historical events in my life, in the previous sections, are narrated to allow my conversation with you to make sense, and hopefully help you understand who I am today and how I got to where I am. This is my personal journey and personal biography. I am proud of my past and my present, and I am so expectant of my future. Let's continue!

"Press forward. Do not stop, do not linger in your journey, but strive for the mark set before you."
~George Whitefield~

Chapter 2

Journey to My Light

As I mentioned in the opening chapter, my country of birth has been unstable as long as I have been living. It has actually been unstable since the 1960s, right after the independence, when the African Hero Patrice Lumumba was murdered. Since then, my people—in particular, my tribe, Banyamulenge—have been deprived of their basic rights until today. Although this is not a history book, it is important to acknowledge the context behind my experience as a young man searching for a better future for myself and my family in a foreign land. Understanding the historical factors that led to my situation can provide valuable perspective to our conversation. At the age of 22, I had lived in 3 different countries and in two continents, and I had lived through life-altering experiences. However, somehow, there was an orchestration that took place to usher me into my next steps of my journey, which would eventually unveil my light.

The day I took my flight to Europe, I felt separated from my people and my country. I did not know what to expect, other than hoping that the grass was greener on that side of the world. I had this burning dream to succeed and change my family tree. I wanted to achieve what my father was not able to achieve, and I made a promise to myself that I would make it in life, no matter what challenges I would encounter along the way.

"As life went on, I came to realize that good as well as bad events in life are all triggers that are meant to push us towards our ultimate purpose in life."

Young Asylum Seeker

On July 17, 2003, I made it to Amsterdam, a foreign land that I had only learned about from the geography books. In my innocence, I thought that all white people spoke either English or French. All White, Western people I had ever seen in Africa, spoke one or the other. Here I was, in a land that was not only strange in culture, people, development, etc., but people spoke a language that I had never heard of. How would I make it in this country? I knew that my brother and lifetime friend, John, was in the country. God willing, I would see him soon.

I claimed my asylum and, in few days, I was settled in a refugee camp in a city called Veldhoven, near Eindhoven, the city of the football club PSV and the Philips Electronics Company. There, I met people from all over the globe with different life aspirations. Life in the refugee camp in the Netherlands was the toughest experience I had ever lived through. For the first time, my whole future in this new country I landed in depended on someone else's decision. Whatever the Dutch immigration office would decide, would determine my future in that country. The timer started and the wait was long.

My only dream was to continue my education. I started learning the new language as I waited for my case to be settled. At the same time, I attended an international church and Bible study, and I also joined the worship team of the same church. There, I made lifetime friends that shared life stories and dreams. I met new families that became part of my life right up till today—family Pelsmaeker, family Standbridge, Bill and Alson, Ronie and Jasmine, just to name a few. These new connections made the new life experience in this new and foreign land digestible.

Veldhoven to Groningen

It had been seven months since I landed in Amsterdam. I was settled in Veldhoven with new connections, and I felt I was fitting in. I now knew how to ride a bike. I was learning a new language and exploring the option to continue my education once I mastered the Dutch language I was part of this international church and felt genuinely connected. Life started making sense in this new home of mine. Despite the difficulties of being a refugee in the Netherlands—not being allowed to study until you get your case sorted out, for instance—at this point, I had made long lasting and meaningful friendships.

The next day, when I went to check my mailbox—this was a common mailbox for all residents in the refugee camp—I saw my name; I had mail. Now, seeing your name on the list could mean one of three things: You either got your approval from the immigration office, you got rejected, or you were being transferred to another location. I went to check my mail, and long and behold, I was being transferred to a city in the northern part of the country, called Groningen. The mail came with a transfer letter and a train ticket to take me there. The next morning, I packed my small suitcase and went to the new center. I did not know that this move was a steppingstone to the next chapter of my life.

"Every change in life prepares you for the next level in your life.
If you don't embrace it, you can miss the train that takes you there."

Not long after I had arrived in Groningen, I received mail again, and this time it was an approval of my case, which officially provided me with permanent residence in the Kingdom of the Netherlands. I immediately registered and restarted my undergraduate education at the University of Groningen, one of the best and oldest universities in Europe. It was, also, in Groningen that I reconnected with John, with whom I shared all and nothing, and I also made other lifetime relationships that made my life meaningful.

Finding a Father

My life in Groningen started making more sense the day I met my sister Jacoline. It was on a Tuesday in a French speaking Bible study, which my friend John had invited me to. During that evening, I connected with this young and vibrant lady, who was typically Dutch but spoke very fluent French. On that evening, we exchanged numbers and we made an appointment to meet on Sunday morning so that she could show me the church she attended. From that day, the rest is history. Jacoline became my sister, and truly a sister to me. She introduced me to her family, who embraced me, and I became a son to Papa and Mama Sterken.

Through a casual conversation with my sister Jaco, on that Tuesday evening, I found a new family—a Dutch, White family that became my family. This became my family to the point that Papa Sterken paid my dowry. Can you imagine a Dutch family paying a wedding dowry? This is what I call becoming a family. Papa Sterken stepped into the role of a father and did it in terms of my culture. There is no such thing in the Dutch culture as a dowry, but Papa Sterken played the role of a father because he wanted to honor his son he had just met a few years back.

Having this family made my life so easy in Groningen. They taught me how to navigate through the system, and whenever anything broke in my house, Papa was there to fix it, while teaching me. I remember that my very first house painting experience was with sister Jaco and brother John. You wouldn't want to be part of that experience. I will just leave it there, for another time maybe!

Education Culture Shock

I was finally settled, and the future seemed clear as I continued with my undergraduate program. Shortly after, the journey at the University of Groningen started to become another big culture shock for me. At first, I wanted to continue with my biochemistry stream, but my Dutch proficiency was not at the required level. So, I changed my orientation and studied International Economics and Business. Not only was this a new field for me, but the education style and methodologies were far from what I was accustomed to.

During my previous education, from elementary to high school, the language was French, and the style was also different. Now, it was in an English education language and the style was more or less self-regulated. The teachers would come and give a forty-five-minute presentation and then leave. The rest was for you to figure out. I was used to a more summarized teaching style, where the teacher would provide a synthesis of the material to focus on. I had to adapt to the new system and way of efficiently studying. The journey became exciting but also challenging, and it did not leave much room for any other life adventure. I, therefore, resolved to make my maximum effort to do well at school—no other plans other than studying and studying and studying! My resolution was to be disrupted and revolutionized as soon as I met my light—disrupted in the sense that I did not stick to it, and revolutionized because once I met my light, my life made sense; I had strong reasons to wake up every day. Her light was so strong that it did not leave me unshaken.

Finding My Light

If you were with me in the introductory paragraphs to this book, that evening with a bunch of other young people who had landed in this foreign land in search for a better future, I had visited my friend John in the suburbs of Groningen, in a city called Leek. I did not know that I would have a revealing telephone conversation that was to change the whole trajectory of my life. I was about to discover the most impactful human being that would make the next 14 years of my life the most memorable ones. Her love and memories shared would forever impact the way I perceive success, purpose, and life in general. What waited for me was about to create that very hope that remains, despite life's dark moments. I had always believed that I would only seriously date the person I would marry, my wife. My encounter with my princess became a self-fulfilling prophecy. After we met, on June 5, 2004, the conviction was spontaneous, and the commitment was firm.

This strangely interesting lady was to impact my life in ways that I could never have imagined. What started with a simple introduction through a mutual friend, was to birth a love story between two young people who were set for a journey full of surprises and wonders, through thick and thin.

In the following chapters, I will journey with you through my love story, my loss of my wife, my grief, and my hope that remains. It is a story of my love for Estelle. It is a story about two souls that were so matched but were separated by a sudden death that almost dimmed the light that we both shared.

My hope is that through our story, you will find reasons to hope again, reasons to love and cherish those in your care, and reasons to be attentive to the light in your own life.

This is the journey to "my light."

PART TWO

FINDING MY LIGHT

"If you find someone you love in your life,
then hang on to that love."
~Princess Diana~

Chapter 3

Loving Estelle, My Light

Plans can change, and they should be flexible enough to change; otherwise, life will cease to exist when we go through life altering events. Although all changes often disrupt our current processes and routines, depending on the nature of the changes, some can be more welcome than others. When you are excited about the change, you get motivated, and you become an active participant in the process. This is what happened to me when my encounter with Estelle took place. I was not reactive to the change; rather, I took an active role to make the change happen. This, however, did not come challenge free. I was, beyond any reasonable doubt, convinced that this strange but out of the ordinary lady was going to be my wife. But how was that going to happen? I resolved to be intentional from day one and remained so in every move thereafter.

My heart was convinced, and my mind was clear. It was time to start talking to Estelle, and my conversation with her was not going to be any sort of purposeless talk. It would be geared towards winning her heart and proposing to her in marriage. Whether it would take years before my proposal materialized was not a question to ask at that point. I was ready to wait, as long as I got her promise. I do remember the first call with my light; I was shaking. She was so calm and welcoming that we talked for hours. They say that your first instinct is always true. It is indeed. As we started spending time talking, before we even met, my conviction became firm: I would marry Estelle one day.

June 5, 2004

It was early in the morning on a Saturday. I packed my guitar and jumped on my bicycle to catch the train from Groningen to Utrecht. I was meeting my friend John, and we were both going for the very first time to attend an African church gathering in a city near Utrecht, called Culemborg. Estelle would be there. I was so excited to be able to see her for the very first time; at the same time, I was freaking out inside. Yes, we had been talking on the phone, but this first meet-up gave me goosebumps—would I contain myself or would I lose control and make it noticeable that I had been drawn to her before I even met her in person? It was a good two-hour trip that seemed to last for months. The train ride was very smooth, and my expectations were very high.

At this point, Estelle knew that I was interested in her, but I had not shared my intentions with her just yet. Since we had been talking on a regular basis, she knew that I would be attending the service that day, which increased the level of my nervousness. It is one thing to meet someone you have started showing signs of being interested in becoming more than just a friend, and it is another thing when the person knows that you will meet at an appointed time. Two hours elapsed before we arrived at the place of the service. We attended the church service, which took a good four hours, during which I had to sing. Imagine that John and I were the new people in a group of close to three hundred people, most of them being young. It felt like all eyes were on us, and the fact that I was to sing while playing my acoustic guitar made the tension skyrocket in my chest. The time came when I was requested to sing, and although I was very nervous, boy, I pulled out my best that day.

After the service, they insisted that I take a few minutes to teach them new songs. I was not prepared for that, but I had to do it anyway. I took my guitar and played the song "Above All" by Lenny LeBlanc. This was a very simple song with very few guitar chords, and it was therefore easy to teach. To my surprise, that was one of Estelle's favorite songs at that time. She sang aloud and harmonized with me as we kind of both taught the rest of the group the song. I came to learn later on that her friends started telling her that this young man was going to be her perfect match. Why? I believe heaven was advocating for me. Not to brag, but there were also a couple of young men who felt very insecure after my appearance.

After the meeting, we finally greeted each other and introduced ourselves. And the intro went like this: "It's you, Estelle?"

It's you, Willy?"

I remember how big my smile was. It just felt so right to be in her presence. Her smile could just melt your heart and, truth be told, it was hard to leave untouched by the contagious warmth that stemmed from the smile Estelle gave everyone who encountered her.

Because she knew that I was interested, she avoided staying with me for long. Instead, she went and talked to my friend John. It did not feel good, I must confess. As smart as she was and very discerning, she did not want to attract unnecessary comments. We walked in, all together, and then back to the train station, and we said our goodbyes. Their train came first, so we stood there and waved to them as they took off. It felt like I was missing someone I had known for so long. In all honesty, I did not want that afternoon to go by so fast. Before we parted at the train station, I told Estelle that I was going to call her later in the evening.

The train towards Groningen came shortly after the one that transported my crush, and we also boarded and started our two-hour ride back home. My trip back to Groningen seemed to last longer than usual. I wanted to get home and call Estelle immediately. I did not want to spend another day before telling her what was in my heart. On our way back, John did not stop teasing me, and I wanted it to continue as it allowed us to talk about Estelle.

I Love You

As soon as I got home, after dinner, I sat in my studio living room, on a one-seater couch, and called my light. She had also safely arrived at her place and was settled in her own room, she said. We talked for a good hour about the day, how it was fun to sing together, and about what we noticed in that long service. I then took a deep breath and broke the ice. I told her that I loved her and that I was not asking for a date but rather for a life commitment. "I want you to be my life partner," I said. She made a joke and laughed about it. After a few minutes, she realized that I was serious, and then she paused and took a deep breath. In those few minutes, I felt like I had jumped a few stairs, but at the same time, it felt good in my heart that I had expressed my deepest feelings.

In her wisdom, she did not push me away but calmly thanked me for expressing myself openly. She then asked me if it was okay to give her some time to think and pray about my request. I confidently responded, saying, "Please take the time you need. Don't feel pressured to give me your answer now. I am not going anywhere; I will wait." I was so convinced in my heart that she was the one I was going to marry that it did not matter how long she would take, as long as we continued talking. I had come out of my comfort zone; I had made the most important statement in my life by asking Estelle to start a love journey that would take us into our marriage for life.

From that very conversation on June 5, 2004, I do not remember a day that passed by without talking to my light on the phone, in a text message, or on Yahoo or Hotmail messenger, the then social media. This was before smart phones, Facebook, WhatsApp, and all social media platforms.

Three Months' Wait

A week had passed since I had made my case. We were talking every single day and were getting to know each other, and the connection was so strong. It became almost impossible to spend a day without talking. I would, from time to time, remind her that she was going to be my wife, to which she would always push back but in a smooth and gallant way. I remember, one day, I purposely did not reach out, to see if she would reach out. She did not call but later on confessed that she could not sleep. The next morning, she called me and asked if I was well. I knew things were turning for my good.

The next day, she called me and asked me to wait for her formal answer after three months. In the back of my mind, I wondered why she asked me to wait for exactly three months. Was she going to make me wait and then come back with a negative answer, I asked myself. At the same time, I consoled myself by thinking that if she was going to say no to my request, she could have said it and maybe limited the interactions we had.

I was not in a rush, and I enjoyed what we were sharing, so it did not bother me that much to patiently wait. As time elapsed, we truly became lovers, even though she had not yet officially given me her word. We asked questions in the quest to know each other better; we shared our dreams and directions we wanted our lives to go in, which attached us even more.

It felt like we knew each other already, and we also started opening up about our lives' secrets.

On September 30,2004, she positively responded to my request. She said, "Yes, I accept your request to share life with you, with conditions: We are not to make our relationship public just yet—only our inner circle of friends and parents should know. Plus, we will never meet in private, just me and you, until we are husband and wife. If you agree to those conditions, you have my word that I will be your wife in due time." I accepted the conditions, and we were set for a good love story. The next day, I took a train and traveled for six hours, back and forth, to meet my fiancée. We sealed our commitment in a prayer after we had spent the whole afternoon enjoying each other's company in the city of Den Helder, where she was living at that time.

Our Dating Guiding Principles

We were officially engaged, and a new chapter of our lives had entered the editing phase. We started communicating as partners in the journey to becoming one. Since September 30, 2004, I had not called Estelle by her name, till the last day (more on this later) when she left for good. Since that day, I called her Princess—and yes, she was the very definition of a princess to me.

We announced our commitment to a few close friends because we wanted to be accountable to those close to us. After a few months, once we had digested and accepted our new status, we decided to tell our parents so that we could get their blessings. We did not want to entertain and develop our relationship without the blessings of our respective parents.

I was the first one to break the news to my mother. I introduced Princess and immediately got a traditional shout of "Impundu" because she was so happy that I had found someone who inspired me so much. This was the very first lady I had ever presented to my mother. She was my first love for life. I received the blessings from my mother, and it made me so glad.

It was now her turn. Now, Princess was so close to her father, in a way I could not explain, to the point that there were things she could simply not allow herself to do—not because they were wrong in essence, but because she knew her father would not appreciate it, even miles and miles away. One of those things was to date. She had promised her dad that she would not date before finishing her education.

I had messed up this plan!

> *"Many are the plans in a person's heart,*
> *but it is the LORD's purpose that prevails."*
> ~ Proverbs 19:21

You will understand later how my encounter with Princess, my light, was meant to save the day in due time.

She called her dad and explained what had happened—how we met and how we connected and the agreements we had in place. I was still studying, and she was also starting that same year, so she assured her papa that we would pursue our studies without any compromise. Her papa gave his blessings, and this was a firm confirmation that we were on a journey till death do us apart. She had clearly told me that she would not continue our relationship should her father not support and give her his blessings. Man, this was a big relief for me. The journey to a life full of good memories was set in motion.

I will not dwell much on our dating period; however, one thing I will share here is that dating Princess transformed my life for the better and for the rest of my life. I would date her now, in this life and the life after, and again and again, simply because it was pure and burdenless when it came to our love for each other.

Firm Commitment

Being a wholehearted person in all my endeavors, I loved Princess without a bit left behind. I was committed to her, to the point that I did not think twice when it came to her. Whenever she would call me and needed to see me, even if I was in class, I would pack up my books and laptop and board a train for a good three-hour ride to her place. We would meet outside to abide by our commitment, and we would spend time together, and then I would always take the last train back to Groningen. Princess, on the other hand, was a very prudent person by nature. Her commitment was firm and meticulously calculated. Contrary to my character, she would, in many cases, sacrifice her happiness to take care of those she cared for. Although she loved me to the maximum, she never wanted to have me take the place of other relationships she had. There were many occasions where I needed her to do something or be with me, but because she had other commitments, she would lovingly say no to me. I knew that I was her number one (after God, of course), and what made me love her even more was the fact that she was calmer when it came to impulses during our courtship period.

I am not suggesting that my commitment was all or nothing; however, I felt compelled to sometimes cancel other priorities because my priority had become her. I did not drop my relationships and other life commitments—far from that—but nevertheless, I had become incapable of prioritizing other things over Princess's attention.

Path to Marriage

The path to our marriage was not a straightforward one, in spite of the fact that our parents had blessed our journey. As time passed, we made our relationship public, and some people did not approve of it, which is normal. You can't expect everyone to be on your side, especially when you are making lifetime decisions. In addition, halfway through our dating journey, as I had just graduated from the University of Groningen and was pursuing my master's degree at the University of Utrecht, and Princess was pursuing her undergraduate at the college of Rotterdam, her residence permit expired and was not renewed. The immigration system in the Netherlands, at least at that time, was very complex. They offered a first 3-year renewable residence after which you had to re-apply; if approved, you would then become a permanent resident. Weird, I know.

Princess had re-applied for her permanent residence status and the answer returned as negative. This meant that she had to appeal, which would take another few months, and sometimes even years, before the institution would respond; if denied, the odds to be expelled from the country would kick in.

"You are happy and hopeful, until the day someone else has the power to decide about your future."

My princess and I had decided that we would finish our studies and travel to Rwanda to celebrate our union in the presence of our beloved families and friends.

So, we waited for her residence to be renewed. One year passed, and towards the second year, she was refused the right to stay in the Netherlands. This period of waiting impacted her right to continue with her study, so she had to put that on hold. We held together, we loved each other more, and we continued to stay true to our initial commitments. At some point, I became angry at the whole situation and the system because I felt helpless as I could not speed up the process.

In the summer of 2009, we prayed and felt convinced that we should no longer wait for the immigration's response before we get married. Princess had a dream wedding she wanted to have, and I had promised to live up to her dreams. One of the requirements she had was to have her mother and siblings around, which is why we wanted to celebrate our marriage in Kigali. We issued invitations for her family and my family to attend the wedding, and as we believed, they all were able to travel to witness our vows. I was finally marrying the love of my life in the presence of many.

WE for Life

On October 23–25, 2009, we united our lives for life, and for better or for worse. The day we had been waiting for, for more than five years, had finally arrived; we were officially and blessedly each other's soul—we had become one. The qualities I had always dreamed of in a wife were all, and even more, personified in who Estelle was. Her love allowed me to leave my past behind and started operating in fulfilled alignment with who we really were as individuals. Our souls drew each other in through a strong spiritual, emotional, and physical connection that set a strong foundation for us to start healing our pasts together. Our union in oneness created a space where we felt safe, whole and complete, heard, and could communicate our thoughts and feelings freely, without the fear of rejection, and most importantly, we felt the ability to be who we really are.

Our wedding was organized in a short period, from July to October. In addition to preparing the ceremony of our dream wedding—I must say, my princess's dream wedding because, for me, it mattered less, as what I wanted was to be brought together in marriage—we also had to invite both our families from Africa. To our surprise, both our mothers, my two brothers, and Princess's sister and uncle—in total, six people—traveled for our wedding from Kigali. This was one of the highlights of our togetherness journey as it did not only color our ceremony, but it also grounded us in the blessings of our parents. It spoke volumes to be able to have our mothers and siblings witness our union and to get their affirmation promptly.

On that day, I realized what it meant to marry your soul mate. Marrying the one you are meant to be with comes with many blessings, despite challenges. Our wedding day was full of testimonies and joy that just overflowed throughout the whole ceremony. Our love that started in humble ways, through immigration challenges, was celebrated on a high note. On Friday the 23rd, we went to the city hall for the civil wedding. It was so fulfilling to solemnly vow before the law in the presence of our mothers that day. Saturday the 24th was the D-day in the presence of many and God. Our belief was, and still is for me, that the marriage would not be valid until it was blessed in the presence of God, through his church. And on Sunday the 25th, we had our final traditional ceremony to unveil the newlyweds—we call this ceremony "Gutwikurura." Mr. and Mrs.

Gakunzi were officially released, by tradition, to go out and start their family. I felt and took pleasure in the weight of my "yes" to Princess, my light; this was the first ever life changing decision I had made, after receiving Christ as my Lord and Savior.

Honeymoon vs Deportation

Life is sweeter than honey when it is shared with the one you love, truly. Best said, when you share and savor the life moments with the one who loves you, truly. I have had so many memorable experiences, both joyful and painful, but when I united with Estelle in holy matrimony, my life was transformed and has never been the same since. I discovered true love and true joy in the harmony of our union and in all dimensions. I discovered for the first time what it really meant to be loved, valued, appreciated, and supported. During our courtship period, I always thought that I had understood what to love and be loved was, but I was not even close. Princess and I truly loved each other and made sure each of us found their space in this new setting called marriage. I felt limitless knowing that Estelle was by my side, despite the material possessions, which were almost nonexistent.

This extraordinary life experience, however, was not void of challenges and, at some point, valid reasons to despair. Six months after our wedding, as life was taking shape as newlyweds full of dreams and plans, and there was a new career path for me in the technology and financial services, we received a letter ordering my wife to leave the country in 25 days. The Dutch immigration office had decided to separate two souls united by law and by God. This came, yet again, as another shock to destabilize our strong and unshakeable love.

This news came at the time when we were shaping our new identity as a couple. Six months of happiness had passed, the two were becoming one, and the path ahead looked straightforward. It came as a poisonous weed in a plantation of white and pink roses in the springtime. Just as the farmer went out to water them, it was realized that the weeds had started suffocating them.

I remember when we sat with our lawyer—wonderful, professional, and compassionate Marieke—in her office in Amsterdam; she looked at me and said, "You have options to prevent this to happen. You are a Dutch citizen, and you have a career; you have two feasible options to choose from."

You can choose to let your wife go back to her country of origin, and you will file a spouse sponsorship case based on your marriage. Or you can decide to move to another European country, find a job there, and apply for your partner's residence permit. She then went on and explained the pros and cons of both options.

Going back to Rwanda meant that we would be separated for a period we both did not know; even the lawyer could not advise on how long the process would take. All would depend on the Dutch immigration office's process duration. It could take months or even years. This was a no-go for me. How can someone, somewhere, just decide to separate me from my light? I had vowed, six months back, that until death do us apart, I would cling to her.

Moving to another European country had its own risks too. We would both have to leave everything we had started building in the Netherlands and embark on an uncertain journey, without a job offer. How would we find a house in a country we do not know much about? And which

European country should we move to? How long would it take for us to settle? I had to make one of the hardest decisions in my life. However hard it was, there was nothing I would not do to save our marriage from breaking. That same day, we decided to move to Belgium, without much there.

> *"Every setback in your life can be a steppingstone to your next level. You just have to take actions in your power and control the controllable in your life."*

We packed the little we could and moved to Belgium. We stayed at our friend's house for a couple of weeks until we found our own apartment to rent. I will not go into every single detail of the moving process; however, we found favor with men as we knocked at different doors, starting with our landlord, who trusted me and accepted for us to rent his apartment when we did not have a stable source of income.

Anchored in the Love

Storms came and the wind blew hard from all corners, right when our new life was starting to take shape. The odds for us to keep moving forward in harmony and love were close to zero, had we focused on what we did not have. This disruption was a recipe for frustration, discontentment, and even a breakup. The reality had hit hard and the requirements to hold hands to navigate through the uncertain and broken hopes were very high for a young couple to attain and maintain.

Fortunately, the heavy rain found us anchored in love for each other and for God. I should say that God loved me so much that he had given me a prayerful partner who would look into my eyes and tell me that everything will be okay. I understood more the importance of a godly woman in one's life when all hopes seemingly disappeared. In the lowest level in our marriage, caused by external factors we did not have control over, I witnessed the power of a wife that stood up to fill the gap. Princess proved to me that she was not going to be there only in our highest moments; she would also make sure she could push me further for the sake of our family. I was doing the easy part, looking for a job in this new country we had moved to, and going out to labor so I could put food on the table. The hardest part during this period of limitation was the ability to maintain the harmony in our marriage and keep the flame burning. I never saw Princess discouraged or worried because of what we were going through. Her mind was sharp, her attitude was always positive, and her dreams never wavered.

Anchored in this strong love we shared, we stood firm with not much to offer in terms of material possession, but our home became a haven for those who did not have much. We were blessed to host people almost every weekend, and we always had enough to share; most importantly, we shared our love. I can, with no shame, boldly say that my family overcame this first trial because of the godly woman I was blessed with. Her love and prayerful life carried us through, and life continued to be sweeter each day that passed.

Hard Labor for Love with a Master's Degree in My Drawer

We had three months to prove that I was legally employed in Belgium, for both my princess and I to get the residence permit. If I failed to get employment, we would run the risk of becoming illegal in Belgium, which would translate into another sort of deportation. I was a Dutch citizen but could not go back with my princess without a valid visa.

In addition to this legal aspect of the matter, we had to survive. There were bills to pay and a family life to sustain. I had just married the most beautiful young lady I had ever seen in my life, but I was in a situation where I could not meet all her needs. It was becoming too much. The little savings we had was starting to dry up, and although I was qualified and could work in Belgium, the job search had been far from yielding any results.

As I continued my job search, I also had to find a way to earn, and the only available job that I could find without any professional credentials was a manufacturing job. So, I started working in a logistic storehouse. I did heavy lifting, manually loading and offloading trucks. I worked early shifts, late shifts, and anything in between. This experience humbled me so much and, at the same time, it drained my energy to the maximum. If I did not have a stable and supporting life partner, I could not have kept the course.

The experience of working in the storehouse made me realize that what mattered most was not my status and education credentials I had earned. However hard it was, it procured me with joy and peace to know that I was playing my part to save and secure my family. I had to provide security and protection for my light. This is the time when our love grew exponentially. We were happier than ever before; not because of what we had, but rather because of what we did not have and the realization of having each other's backs. We knew that nothing and no one could separate us as long as we were fulfilled with the joy that our love provided.

I continued doing the hard labor until I was able to re-enter the professional market. It was not easy to balance between the survival jobs and my career job search. I had so many rejections; most of them were biased because of racial reasons, to the point that I decided to never go for a job interview. This happened after I had an interview with a renowned multinational technology company, and the hiring manager openly told me that he would not hire me because their customers had not yet embraced diversity. I was devastated and decided to never attend any interview. Two weeks later, I received a call from a hiring manager at BTR Services, and he offered me a job without a formal interview. The same pattern continued a few years later when I was again called by a recruiter that led me to my current job. It was also an offer that I had not applied for. I did attend interviews, but this time it was different. Wolters Kluwer is the place to be when you have to be right. After a decade in service with this company, I am still growing and satisfied.

Prepared in the Wilderness

During this transition period of finding a legal refuge for my family's stability, my career was altered, and our family's future was at stake. As I went out to hunt for survival needs, it moved me further from the professional market. My experience and education credentials were becoming outdated. I decided to take new courses in information technology, as a business architect. This was a big shift that took my competence to another level, while I continued to do the heavy job to provide for my family.

However difficult it was—dealing with the legal immigration requirements, keeping the family standards and values in check, and taking a new course—I strongly believed, and still do, in a positive correlation between competence, opportunity, and increase in life. By the time I finally broke through the employment discrimination I had endured for a while, I was ready to deliver and go up the ladder at a short and speedy pace. Yes, during that transition phase, we lacked financially, but at the same time, we sustained our family equilibrium, and I was able to continue upgrading my competence while waiting for the opportunity to match.

It would not have been possible if I did not have a supportive wife and a strong believer in my ability. As I said earlier, she was the first person who saw the lion inside of me and spoke it into existence. She never ceased to believe and affirm my potential. She provided a safe and loving home to look forward to going to after every hard day of laboring and job hunting, and that empowered me to soar even higher.

Stronger Together

Our humble beginnings did not diminish or impact the increasing trajectory of our love. We were not the perfect couple; however, our lifestyle perfectly harmonized and continued in the growth path amidst the challenges we faced. We kept doing that small, next right thing in our lives without necessarily approaching life from a big bang approach. The more we kept moving, the deeper our love grew, and the less probable the friction would happen. Without much effort, we realized that we had built strong habits that sustained our love steadily. We did not plan to implement anything as such; rather, we did what we felt was good for us, what was deepening our connections at all levels, and that which provided joy on a daily basis. Before we knew it, we had formed new habits that allowed our marriage to flourish amidst the life challenges we had gone through. A few habits stood out and strengthened our love even after (more in the later chapter) the light got dimmer:

LOVE LETTER – Prior to our marriage, we would text and send each other letters regularly. From the day we got married, without a formal discussion, we started writing each other love notes before leaving the house. It became one of the easiest ways to appreciate, to encourage, and to affirm each other on a daily basis. We found ourselves replacing the text messages we were exchanging as fiancés, with love letters to each other every day. We then bought notebooks and we continued writing each other love letters every single day. Every morning when we woke up, we would read each other's letters before anything else.

When we moved—rather, when we were forced to move—from the Netherlands to Belgium, this habit was strengthened. A lot was going on that required our energy and focus as we navigated this disruptive change, and so we needed to ground ourselves in love and intentional acts of love. In addition to doing all the other things married couples would do to support and encourage each other, our love letters best expressed what we needed.

Because I was working shift schedules, Princess would write her letters before bedtime for me to read early in the morning before I headed out for a heavy working day. I would then write my love letter in the morning before leaving home, and she would read it when she woke up. Reading her words of affirmation and love every morning was recharging. Nothing could happen on any given day that would challenge me enough to disrupt my performance or trigger a mood swing. I felt so much love and support, to the point that I would find my mindset already sharpened. This practice in itself was a recipe for a successful marriage, regardless of the material limitation we had back then.

SINGING, DANCING, AND PLAYING TOGETHER – Our second pillar we built our marriage on was to sing, play, and dance together.

We sang while driving, in the shower, while making dinner, etc. When it came to dancing, Princess was an expert in all genres. She would come up with moves and swings just to make fun of me, and then she would challenge me to do the same. Then we would pick from there and just enjoy each other through dancing. Oh, how we loved dancing to zouk and slow music.

At the same time, after my light came into my life, that's when I started writing my own songs. We both loved singing gospel songs, so every evening, we took time to sing together. We also made sure that we had play time and dance time on a regular basis. As our bond became stronger and stronger, we started writing songs together. There is power when a couple harmonizes in melody; it trickles down to other areas of their lives. We lived this wonderful experience day in and day out.

PRAYING TOGETHER – Our third and most important habit we developed way before our marriage was praying together—not praying in solo for each other, but praying together, holding hands, and hugging if necessary. We had our family prayer meeting every evening at 7 p.m., after dinner, where we took time to pray for each other, hand in hand. We literally prayed for everything—everything you can think of that happens in a family and couple setting was a subject of prayer for us. This increased our intimacy with God and with each other. I will not take any credit for this habit. If it had not been for Princess's heart for God and consistency in prayer, I am not sure I would have sustained it myself. She lit my life in so many ways.

SERVING PEOPLE – For those who know me, although very reserved, I am a very social person but an introvert at the same time. I am an introvert in the sense that I hardly open up. It takes time and firm trust for me to open up. My light, on the other hand, was very social and discreet.

She was that trusted friend that made everyone feel like their best friend; everyone who encountered her thought that they were the only friend she had. Whenever everyone would be around, she would manage to attend to everyone's needs as a friend, without making anyone feel more attached than the other. Every friend of hers thought that they were her best friend. In her discretion, she never wanted to take any credit for the things she would do for anyone. In many cases, she would work in the background and let either me or any other friend be the face of the initiative.

We nurtured this culture in our home, and we became the resting shoulders for many. I can hardly remember any weekend we spent without hosting people in our home. Those who had enough and those who were lacking, were all welcome. We had made our minds up, as a family, to be a reason for someone's smile whenever the opportunity presented itself.

I came to realize that happiness in love is not always positively correlated with material possessions. I loved Estelle, my light, and I know she loved me deeply, even when we were lacking. As our love flourished, other aspects of our lives expanded and increased.

Intentionality

I strongly believe that love goes through different stages before it matures. The first stage, which we all refer to as the "falling in love" stage, is essentially an emotional and intense feelings stage where everything seems flawless. There are no questions asked because, when we are in the presence of the one we love at that stage, the rest seems to disappear in our rational sight. At this stage, promises can be easily made, and all dreams seem attainable, altogether. At this stage, we are less discerning as all we want to do is to be with the person we are in love with. This stage, in my view, is the trigger of every love journey. When not handled wisely, this beautiful experience can be detrimental, and love feelings can turn into a bitter drink.

The second stage in this journey we call love is what I call "facing reality." At this stage, eyes are opened, and you start to see the flaws and what you do not like about the person you love. You realize that this individual, who is capable of awakening the inner sensations you did not know were in you, can also fall short. You start realizing that your power can clash, and when it happens, the personal defense mechanism is called on to rescue you. You now know that she/he can miss the appointment. She/he can be late. She/he can irritate you. This realization impacts your feelings for the person you love and have declared time and time again that you will never see any less of them. You start to even wonder how in the world you could end up falling for someone with so many flaws. Comparison kicks in, and you start seeing better options out there. At this point, you have reached a turning point; you either resolve to make it happen or you break the beautiful treasure in the making.

The third stage, the "mature" stage, is the intentional level of love. You have navigated through your feelings and the reality check. You have managed to regulate all those chemicals that cause positive and negative friction. At this stage, you intentionally decide to fly high like an airplane that has reached a ground roll (takeoff roll) stage, which is the portion of the takeoff procedure where an airplane accelerates from a standstill to an airspeed that provides sufficient lift to become airborne. At this level, the plane's wings receive enough power to lift the heavy weight of the huge machine above the surface.

This is exactly what happens in the matter of love. Long lasting and fulfilled relationships are intentional, where two people daily choose to commit to each other despite their respective flaws. Yes, my relationship with my light was not absent of challenges caused by both external factors and personality difference. Amidst all, we intentionally committed to each other earlier in our journey. We had made a commitment to never allow our differences and life challenges to impact the initial motivation of engaging in our life journey together. Here are some of the tools we implemented early on in our love journey:

Apologize and forgive always – There was nothing we could not apologize for and forgive each other for.

Pray together every day – We resolved to pray together no matter what, and after a fight—yes, we had fights—there was no excuse not to pray together and in a loud voice. Even when I was traveling for work, we had time to pray together and affirm each other.

I love you – We resolved to remind each other of our love every morning and before going to bed.

Kiss – Before going out, when returning home, and before going to bed, we were indebted to give each other a kiss on the cheek, forehead, or lips.

Hand in hand – We resolved to hold hands whenever we sat down; we held hands while driving, we held hands in church, we held hands while resting at home—we held hands whenever we were around each other. Of course, we were a very respectful couple, so whenever the environment did not allow us to hold hands, we always complied.

Check-in – Whenever we were apart, it was automatic to send each other small and short check-in text messages throughout the day. In fact, the last message she texted me, in French, when she arrived at work, said:

"Hi honey, I arrived safe at work. May the Lord God give you strength in everything. I love you."

I strongly believe that romance and feelings can grow strong through the different stages of a love relationship between a husband and wife if they are cemented with strong communication and self-giving. I signed off from day one, and so did Princess, that we would do our best to provide each other space for self-love and growth. By providing space to be ourselves, it allowed us to serve each other with grace. I always strived to provide security, making sure she was provided with enough love and cover in all aspects of her life to the best of my abilities, and she always strived to give me space to see light that allowed me to continue growing in love and increase in our fulfillment.

My love journey with my princess had, this far, been tried and came out stronger. We had achieved peace and fulfillment that translated into living in abundance, even when we were lacking material possessions. We also understood that contentment is found in serving others with our lives.

The Power of Consecration as a Couple – Lasting Legacy

After a season in the desert, financially lacking and doing the hard labor as we settled in our new home country, God had come, and he had seen us through. The drought was over. We were able to dream again and our plans as a new couple were within our reach.

When I finally got back to my professional employment, it was such a blessing that provided not only peace of mind and the financial aspect of it, but it came with extra benefits, including a company car and much more. I understand, to some of you this might sound like business as usual, but if you really think about it, having some of the basic necessities covered can take you a long way in terms of financial soundness.

As a symbol of gratitude to our creator, we vowed to sacrifice the most expensive possession we owned by then, and that was our car. Yes, we bought it as a used car, but it was like new. Although I was given a company car, we still had the option to keep the second car or cash it out and use the money for other projects. To honor our vow, we sold the car and used every euro that we yielded from the sale and donated it to our home church.

We actually wanted to make something that would be a sign that would constantly remind us of how far God had brought us—a place where our education credentials could not but his grace did. So, we took all the money and bought a brand-new professional video camera for the church.

This happened to be the very first professional camera that our church had ever owned. Because of this sacrificial act, our church started recording services and events, which would be uploaded to different social media platforms and broadcasted across the globe.

I still remember how it felt when we held hands as we swiped our bank card, paying for that purchase in the electronic shop in Antwerp, Belgium. We brought the camera to church without telling anyone, and we laid it at the alter as a constant reminder to our God and life situation that we would never be in financial lack again. From that day, we made our minds up that our yesterday would never be better than our today, and our future would always be better than our today and yesterday combined. The journey ahead was ever straight, and there was no going back to the state of lack, especially the lack of peace and contentment.

Before we transition to the second part of the book, where I found myself without my light around, in the next chapter, I will walk you through our life as parents. This is a phase that I believe every parent can identify with. It transforms the lives of parents into another level of accountability, which can grow their love, if well discerned, or can distort their love.

"I'm a father; that's what matters most.
Nothing matters more."
~Gordon Brown~

Chapter 4

A Father to Daughters

Growing up without a father had created a sense of insecurity about my own fatherhood. In many instances, inside, what we fear lies in the strength we carry without us realizing. If you find yourself struggling in any particular area, I encourage you to dig deep down within. You will be surprised to realize how resilient you are. Once you take appropriate actions, the results are mesmerizing. In this chapter, I will share with you how the fear of becoming a father haunted me for so long because I grew up without one myself. I ended up finding my greatest pleasure and strength in fatherhood. Let's turn the page together!

I also did not have the opportunity to have a blood sister. Growing up with only boys in the house was tough and did not provide me with the experience of how to deal with females—sisters or daughters. The fatherless state I grew up in, combined with not having a blood sister, accentuated my insecurity about being a father to daughters. I did not know what to expect as a father in general, and a father to daughters in particular.

So, when I met my light, I wholeheartedly gave my love to the point that I also wondered if my love tank had emptied. This, too, created a sense of uncertainty and fear within me. I wondered if I would be able to love my kids enough, especially since I had no model to emulate. On top of lacking a father figure and sister in my life, being the second to last born in my family meant that I did not have any experience with babies. My younger brother is only two years younger than me. The babies I ever interacted with were my nephews and nieces, but I was young and never babysat them.

All these parameters contributed to creating a sense of scariness that I could not express. I never shared my insecurity with anyone, including Estelle. I kept this fear to myself, and I do not think anyone would have noticed.

One day, in the summer of 2010, I came back home from work and found my princess waiting for me, well dressed in a long purple dress, as though she was attending a ceremony. As I proceeded to the living room, I was welcomed by a dinner table, candles, and slow music playing. A lot of questions popped into my mind; I did not know what was happening. She welcomed me as we normally would do, and then she asked me to go to the room and change and come back to the living room. I took a quick shower, dressed in a similar color she had already prepared, and in a few minutes, I was back but still wondering what was going to happen. I did not have a clue.

We sat at the table, and there was a sealed envelope. She held my hands and asked me how my day was, and then she asked if she could say a prayer before she let me open the envelope. The prayer was not grace for the dinner but rather thanksgiving for the many blessings in our lives. I was so impatient to finish and find out what was in that sealed envelope. When I opened it, the message read: "You are becoming a dad." What followed, I cannot detail enough.

I jumped with joy that I had never experienced in my life. Those who have been blessed with this gift of being a father, the same as being a mother, can relate even though feelings are expressed in different ways. My previous fear turned into unexplainable joy and a sense of responsibility. I even fell in love with Princess more; this wonderful soul was making me be what I had not been able to get. How can you explain that? I literally felt the weight coming off my shoulders, and I could not wait to be a father. Thank you, Princess, for this priceless gift.

Save Him; He Is Short of Oxygen!

The whole summer was very exciting; I would check in every second to see how the baby was growing. It was just such an amazing feeling.

One Saturday morning in September 2010, we were preparing to attend our friend's wedding in the Netherlands. We were going for a one-and-a-half hour drive from Antwerp to Utrecht. This was going to be a surprise for the newlyweds and other friends we were about to meet; we were going to announce our pregnancy to them. We had been pregnant for almost 12 weeks; the first trimester was almost over. There had not been any complications whatsoever, not even morning sickness. It was a very smooth first trimester.

That morning, Princess started getting cramps but did not think it was a big deal. As time passed, the pain intensified. We then decided to call our physician, whose office was one block away from our house. Since the clinic was on our way to the Netherlands, we decided to get ready, pass by his office for a quick check-up, and then continue on to the wedding. By the time we got to the family physician's office, Princess was in too much pain. I inquired if she thought that there was something wrong with the baby (not a very good question to ask, but I guess the adrenaline was high). By default, her nature was calm and very assertive, and she calmed me. She assured me that she was good and that the baby was fine. She said that it was maybe something she had not digested well.

As soon as we entered, the doctor checked her, and I could see that something was not right. She was in so much pain anytime the doctor touched her belly. The excitement I had at becoming a father turned into confusion; I just could not fathom that we might be losing the first fruit of our union. He looked at me and said, "Did you come by car or walk here?" I responded in a shaky voice that we had driven there. Then he said, "Go quickly to the clinic. Your wife and baby need to be checked." I inquired if something wrong had happened. "Is the baby alive; is my wife in danger?" He responded, as a medical professional, "Go to the clinic. They need to quickly take care of your wife."

I do not remember how fast I drove, but I do know that I did not respect the speed limits. The clinic was a five-to-ten-minute drive, and as soon as I pulled over, I opened the door and held Princess's hand and rushed in. We were immediately admitted; however, it was too late. We were losing our baby before we had even met him/her. I could see what was happening, but my brain had not yet comprehended it, so I kept asking if it did really happen.

As the medical staff were helping my wife, who was way calmer than I was, the next thing I do remember was the sound of the doctor screaming, "Sir, stay with us. Can you see my hands?" I could hear a fading sound, but I could not clearly see him. I was on the ground, unconscious. I had fainted due to lack of oxygen in my brain. Apparently, when we are under shock and our blood flow gets distorted, oxygenated blood does not reach the brain. When the level of oxygen is low, the brain will not send nerve signals throughout the body. In as short as a five-minute time frame, cells start dying, causing fainting, unclear vision, seizures, etc. We basically start entering into a deep state of unconsciousness, and if unattended, it can cause permanent damage or even death.

The attention was deviated from Princess to save my life. Thank goodness, I was in good hands, and in the next few minutes, I was back to my conscious state, but I was still troubled within. We had lost our baby that we had never met. Princess was still in pain, but in the short period of half an hour, she had been well taken care of and the pain had reduced. We stayed at the clinic for about three to four hours, and we were then released to go home.

Kayla – Imfura

After the unfortunate event that had happened the previous year, God favored us, and we conceived within the few months that followed. I remember the day Princess announced the news to me; the feelings were mixed. I was overjoyed that the hope of becoming parents was within our reach, but at the same time, I shook from within because of what had happened few months before. The next 12 weeks seemed longer than the whole pregnancy period. I requested that Princess just rest and do nothing, because I was just terrified of going through the same experience again. Thank goodness, the same as the first pregnancy, there were no complications whatsoever. The process was enjoyable and smooth; however, because of what we had experienced, I did live with some level of anxiety through the first trimester.

The first day we went for an ultrasound was mesmerizing. I could hear Kayla's heartbeat. It felt as if a heavy weight was lifted off my shoulders, and the anxiety turned into tears of joy. From that very moment, I felt what it meant to be a father. I was so impatient to finally meet my daughter and to hold her. I really started missing the day she would be there with us in a tangible way.

Thursday, July 28, 2011, at 11:47 a.m., we became parents. Imfura (first-born) was born. What this experience of finally becoming parents gave me cannot be expressed in the few sentences in this section. I did not know what it meant to be called Father before that, but as soon as I cut the umbilical cord, all the pieces came together. I felt complete, I felt so proud, I felt blessed, and most importantly, I felt so much love, respect, and reverence for my Princess, who not only made me a father but also went through the experience of giving life to our Imfura.

As we were preparing to welcome our Imfura, we prayed, we talked, and we did research on names. We wanted to call our children meaningful names. While researching and reaching out to family and friends we trusted, we prayerfully agreed to call our first-born Kayla, meaning "who is like God." It is a name derived from the archangel who is closest to God, archangel Michael. Who could make us parents after the unfortunate event we had gone through the year before? Through Kayla, we saw God's likeness in mercy.

From the day Kayla was born, she stole my heart. Her mother and I bestowed all our love on her without leaving anything behind. In addition, her birth brought tremendous changes to our family life. I was promoted in my job, and we moved to a bigger and better house as we were financially sounder. And, most importantly, we bonded on another level we did not think we had reached yet. The love and commitment I had for Estelle exponentially increased. The next four years that followed were the best, to the point that I did not think that there would be more levels of joy to attain in life.

Shayna – Miracle Baby

The time was right. After almost four years of parenthood, we trusted God for a second blessing. While we prayed and trusted for the second miracle to happen, I was kind of reliving another sort of fear and anxiety. This time, it was not because I did not know how to be and feel like a father. I was scared that I might not have as much love for the second born as I had for the first born. What if I was not able to show the same love? Kayla turned four when we were expecting Shayna, which meant that she was a full human being with expressions. She was monopolizing the house atmosphere; all the attention was on her, and she already knew what she wanted as a child.

This question of how I would be a loving parent to my two kids haunted me for some time, actually until Shayna was born. During the pregnancy, I would ask Princess if she thought I would be able to live up to the task, and she couldn't understand why I was so frightened. Now, for those who have had the opportunity to know who Estelle was, she was the calmest and most stable person you could think of. She knew how to handle different emotions without losing focus. So, she affirmed to me, time and time again, how I was an amazing father, and she was so proud and happy that her daughters had me as their dad.

Now, Shayna came as a miracle baby. Of course, her sister was a miracle, and all babies are miracles from the creator. However, Shayna was a miracle in all sense of the word. During her pregnancy, the doctors noticed that Princess had developed some cardio deficiencies. She had developed a deficiency that they suspected might have originated from the first pregnancy that was lost, or it could have even been there before, without noticing. This added pressure to both of us, and to some degree accentuated my anxiety. I was so terrified that Princess and Shayna were not going to make it.

The pregnancy and the mother's health were without any complications; however, doctors—God bless medical people—wanted to eliminate all risks and strictly followed us on a regular basis. This experience was not the best anyone would want to go through. Instead of having the monthly check-ins, we had check-ins every two weeks, which became so traumatizing to me. As a father and husband, I was limited to what I could do; I only observed and prayed.

On Friday, November 13, 2015, at 4 p.m., Shayna was born. As we prayed and decided on her name, we felt convinced to stay in the same light as her sister. Because God is unique and like no one else, we chose Shayna, which means "God is gracious" and "beautiful." The name just signified who this gorgeous baby was—beautiful inside and out and gracious in all sense of the word. As I beheld her when she was born, I was mesmerized by the power of love that I felt. I mean, Shayna stirred another level of love that I did not think I had left in me.

The love I feared I had bestowed on Kayla, came in intense measures, and at the same time, it did not diminish anything from what was there, both for Kayla and their mother. Shayna was born in a miraculous way, defying medical expectations.

Our family of four continued to be blessed. One year before Shayna's birth, I changed my job and received a promotion that allowed us to have Princess stay at home and care for our daughters. The miraculous baby came with abundant blessings that saw our family reach higher levels in different dimensions of our family life. Although we did not have much extra in financial resources, we had enough abundance to live the life we desired; in many instances, our cup overflowed to serve others.

I Still Love You, Princess

Those who are fortunate to have daughters in their lives will understand me more. I am not suggesting that having sons would be different, not at all. However, from my experience, I believe that if not kept in balance and checked, daughters can easily take over a father's love and cause imbalances for the couple. I soon realized that by being a father, especially a father to daughters, you might not always get it right 100 percent of the time. You need to provide for the family, which equates to not having enough time to care for your lover. On the other hand, if you give all your time, it becomes almost impossible to provide the requisite level of provision. These opposing demands, combined with having three ladies—the mother and daughters—if not kept in check, can soon become a problem.

Princess and I resolved to keep each other in constant check so as not to allow our blessings to take our attention from each other. I must confess here that I had to be constantly reminded of my responsibilities, especially during the early stages of our daughters. I quickly realized that the best way to love my daughters was to intentionally increase my love for their mother.

"One of the best gifts you can give your children is to love their mother."

We did not stop our regular dates, dances, praying together, and holding hands as we initially did, or checking-in, writing love letters, and giving each other kisses in the presence of our children. We resolved to show our children the love we had for each other, even when they were just babies. I will touch on this in the following chapters in detail; however, I came to understand later on that our souls knew that these years were what we had together. I did not learn it from my parents, and I am sure Princess did not learn anything of the like from her parents either; but somehow, our creator compelled us to act the way we acted, and I saw the fruit of that even after I carried on the task by myself. We will explore this in detail in the second part of the book.

"Efforts and courage are not enough
without purpose and direction."
~John F. Kennedy~

Chapter 5

Light Journey to Final and New Destination

After two years in my position at Wolters Kluwer, with intense travel, we were offered the opportunity to relocate to Toronto, Canada. This came as a total surprise. We had not had any active projects in Canada for over three years, and suddenly this opportunity came up and I was selected to take the project. After a few months of back and forth between Toronto and Brussels, my manager and I agreed that the best way was for me to relocate. I later understood that all this was heavenly orchestrated. Toronto was going to be the place where my life and that of my family would experience a disruptive change for the rest of our days.

I was still on a long journey; this time with my light and the fruits of our love, to yet another new land that would be a beckoning of blessings that we had never imagined, on the one hand. On the other hand, it would be a place where we were to experience a disruptive life event that would mark our lives forever.

Dreams we never imagined possible were to unfold in front of our very eyes and at a speedy pace that I had ever thought possible. The former refugees and deported couple were set for a journey that would see them sit with corporate leaders and advise the wise. Everything was happening so fast that we didn't have much time to process it. It seemed too good to be true.

The sequence of events was beyond our own comprehension, and the materialization of outcomes was far beyond anything we had ever planned or imagined in our lives. My background and that of my princess did not correlate with the life we were entering as we journeyed to the place we were to settle in as a new home for our family.

On Another Journey

It was time to travel again, to move to another country, and not only with Princess but also with our two daughters. In 2010, I decided to travel from Utrecht in the Netherlands, with my newly wedded bride, in the hope of finding refuge in the neighboring country, Belgium. Although there were no physical borders with border control officers, it was very dangerous to travel across countries without legal papers of identification. There would be random controls, and if you were not in a legal state, you would face severe consequences, including imprisonment and deportation where possible. The Dutch immigration services had not left me with any other option but to take the risk and drive my secondhand Ford Escort car with my princess, in the hope that we would get to the other side peacefully.

This time, we were traveling intercontinental, legally and as experts. I had been traveling between Brussels and Toronto for work for a period of 6 months. I was constantly jetlagged, and the traveling was taking a toll on my body and my family dynamics. I was missing my daughters' milestones, and it didn't feel good. I remember that the first day Shayne started eating solid food, I was in Toronto, and we facetimed for me to be part of this big event. My career opportunity was becoming a challenge to manage; however, we did not complain and I had Princess's full support.

Suddenly, my manager suggested that I should transfer and move over to Canada with my family. This was to ensure that both work and family life would not be in jeopardy. I remember calling Princess as I was on my way to the airport, traveling back to Brussels. I said, "Honey, I am on my way, but please get ready. We will all come back together." She thought I was joking at first, but that was it; we were set to relocate.

On April 29, 2016, we elegantly and proudly boarded the flight to Toronto as a happy family of four. The difference between this trip and that of July 2010, was not only that the family had expanded, but we also traveled as experts going to provide specialized services to important global systemic financial institutions. We landed in Toronto, a beautiful and big city; we had never seen anything like it before. (I had been here before, but as a family, this was the first time to be in such a big city.)

We spent the next two years living as diplomates. I must say that life and God had prepared a table in the eyes of many. The former refugee, who graduated, had to move to a different country, and could not easily join the labor market because of discrimination, with a family that was almost separated because of their residence status in the Netherlands, was hosted in Toronto with his young family, and was providing expert solutions to global player financial institutions.

Life was too good to be true, as they say. We had shifted to another dimension in life. We had indeed prospered. The two years that followed, from 2016 to November 2018, were years that were restored to us. It felt like the hardship we had gone through had all faded away. I felt like a king who truly provided for his queen and princesses in his kingdom.

I was able to offer a life standard that I had not been able to offer before. In other words, that I had never thought I would be able to offer to those I loved o much. My light lived her last two years fulfilled. She was able to go back to school and finish her college education because we were able to pay by ourselves. We were able to employ a nanny for our babies, which allowed Princess to do other things she loved doing, and I continued my work with peace of mind. She was able to just enjoy life and pursue her life dreams. Thank you for allowing me to make you happy!

Promises Kept

One of the beauties of a love story is the promises and dreams shared for the future. You dream of a world where everything will come to pass and without any hindrances! Princess and I had plans to live those dreams, and I had promised to make them come true, as a man. One of the promises was to travel to places to discover together. What I did not understand back then was the importance of time, the "right now" time. I thought that I had all time on my side; I thought the stretch was long enough and we would get enough of it in the future.

As reality hit and our family expanded, our plans started shifting. Other priorities took precedence to traveling and discovering. As time passed, I realized that time was not a commodity I could bank on for future use. It had to be spent there and now. I realized that time is a commodity that has a very short expiration period, and it is therefore to be consumed in the present and not with the "do it later" mentality.

Lo and behold, God knows how much time we have, and he hears prayers and answers them in the right time. It comes to us to either recognize and use the time and its blessings well, or the cycle passes by. When we moved to Canada through my work transfer, the opportunity to do what we had not been able to do, presented itself. We were financially stable, and our daughters were still young without mandatory attendance at school. Without really planning to do lots of traveling and discovering, we found ourselves doing so. We traveled to places we had not been to; we enjoyed our two years' staycation, where we lived a life we had never imagined we would be able to live.

It dawned on me, after Princess had transitioned, how we were able to package many years of life into a period of two years, and we were able to reach some of our wildest dreams in her lifetime. I then understood the statement made by Martin Luther King: "There are two days in our calendars: today and the day of judgement where we will give account of everything."

Embracing today's opportunity in its entirety has since then become my mantra. I will continue to live by this principle to the best of my abilities until I get hold of the second day on my calendar.

Princess Is Back to School

The hope deferred makes the heart sick, but a longing fulfilled is a tree of life. When you dream and hope to achieve something, especially when you know you have the potential to achieve what you hope for, and it is not reached, it can make even the cheerful and naturally happy person's heart unfulfilled. However, when the desire of our heart is fulfilled, it becomes a tree from which streams of living water spring.

Princess had dropped her college education because of the immigration challenges in the Netherlands, when her residence permit was not renewed. She could not continue with her studies. Looking back, it took a resilient mindset to happily continue to pursue other life's dreams after being forced to drop her education halfway. After forcefully moving to Belgium, we ended up postponing her 2 years that were left to finish her college as the family dynamics evolved. We decided to prioritize our family balance as I was earning well and I later on started traveling for work. This was a sacrificial love for her to defer some of her dreams for the sake of our family's stability.

When we settled in Toronto, expanded and stable as a family, she went back to school to finish college. She went on studying computer engineering in software testing at All Canadian College. After all courses were done, she was placed as an intern. During that period, she found a job with an insurance company in Toronto. Everything was just coming into place. Life was just as we had wanted it to be, and it felt like all our prayers were answered and more was given to us. I was earning extremely well, my princess had done what she always wanted to do and had finished her college education, and our little ones were growing well and healthy, and in an environment we wanted them to grow in. What could possibly go wrong? We were living our dream. Our life was literally fulfilled.

Finding My Life Purpose

We are the sum of life events and experiences that have shaped us in one way or another. On the one hand, our background, culture, and life exposures can build us up to becoming a staircase we use to discover and reach our life purpose. These life events, on the other hand, can also be the barriers to our progress and therefore hinder us from reaching our full potential.

Growing up, as a boy and fatherless, I did not experience any sort of affirmative love as we know today. Boys in general, and in my culture in particular, are expected to be tough, not show their emotions, and to man-up fast. This cultural bias in my case does not mean to say that love was not there; the contrary is true. Love, and I would say genuine love, was there and could be felt.

Yes, I grew up in a loving environment; however, the love was not affirmatively expressed. In my culture, love is not verbally expressed, especially when it comes to boys. With this cultural context and having grown up with only male siblings, our love expression was mainly through soccer (football) and fight games. I knew that my mother and my big brothers were there for me all the time, and they loved me so much; however, I did not know that we can explicitly express our love to each other. I was not exposed to expressive and affirmative love.

When I traveled and got exposed to other cultures, and especially when I met my light, I discovered my emotional and love language to be words of affirmation. When we were courting as fiancées, and especially after we had become one through marriage, I understood what I was most lacking— I was always starved for words of affirmation. I realized that whenever she expressed her support for me—whenever she commended me for a task accomplished, whenever she complimented me, whenever she looked into my eyes and said the words "I LOVE you—I became UNSTOPPABLE. I literally discovered my inner strength, and to a larger degree, my self-worth, through the affirmation that my light provided.

This is something that Princess got to pull out of me. She was the first person to openly affirm me. She believed in me even when I thought I could not make it, which made me go extra miles and actually make it. Her love's expression to me was so affirmative from the day we entered our relationship that my life turned around 180 degrees. I became more compassionate, hardworking, intensely focused, and more socially involved.

I did not know that I could be a good husband because I did not have a model; I had been raised by a single mother. Princess made me a good husband. I did not know that I had hidden talents, such as composing songs, counseling, and mentoring. Princess saw that in me; she affirmed it and helped me grow into that. I wrote my very first song after she said yes to our love journey; after that, the talent expanded and we started writing songs together.

It is often said that we give what we need or what we have, and it is so true. Those close to me can easily affirm to that; I find myself affirming people without realizing that I am doing so. I am an affirmative person (my strongest love language).

Having shared my love and life with Estelle is the most impactful experience of my life till today. Princess was not just a wife to me; she was my best friend, and most importantly, she was my destiny helper. I do not recall deciding anything without consulting her, since we started dating. I can testify that God and life put people in our lives for our benefit. People in our lives are there to usher us into a journey towards our life purpose.

"Living a life with your spouse in perfect harmony is achievable, even in today's era. Ignoring that is robbing life from your life. Failing to strive for it is irresponsibility."

I have lived a fulfilled life in my marriage to Estelle, and I have discovered my life purpose. True love is possible. At the highlight of my life, when all seemed to come together, the light I had encountered dimmed. In the glorious phase of my life, all life's odds seemed to race against me, and my foundations were once again shaken, but this time it was outside my controllable parameters. My light faded away.

When my light faded, I was at the lowest point of my life. What I didn't understand at the time was how, by that same light, I would be able to stand tall and eventually testify that even when light fades away, hope remains. Even in the physical absence of the light, daring to love, daring to believe, daring to hope, and daring to rise and collect pieces is still possible. Let's turn to the next section of this memoire.

PART THREE

WHEN LIGHT FADES AWAY

"My most brilliant achievement was my ability to be able to persuade my wife to marry me."
~Winston Churchill~

Chapter 6

When Light Fades Away

"If today is the last day you are going to see Estelle alive, what will you say and how will you behave? How about the dreams and plans you share? What will you do with them? Will you let them be silenced with her?" This was the strange conversation that happened between me and an invisible voice in the back seat of my car as I drove down highway 401, from North York in Toronto to downtown, after I had received the call that Princess had been rushed to the hospital, on Thursday, November 8, 2018, around 4:30 p.m.

Without comprehending what was ahead of me that night, my soul and my mind were already preparing. The man within had already read the message written in my next life's chapter that was about to be opened; this would be a chapter of pain and grief, a journey of life through tears and toils as life's darkest night had arrived.

It would be known to all, and it would shake and turn my world upside down—this chapter I had never dreamed about and never wished to read. This is the chapter I would rather read as part of fiction and unreal scenarized plays. It's a chapter that I would by no means wish to see unveiled in the lives of those you love and care for. It is, indeed, a chapter of the book that no human being should have to read in their lifetime.

Unfortunately, at this point, I had already seen this chapter unfold in the lives of those I loved so much, including my own mother. The words of the wise resonate still: "Nothing is new under the heavens; what has been will always be." The circle of life had reached my roundabout and it had decided to knock on the door of my house. The light was about to dim, yet the life journey would continue. Will the source of light extinguish its luminosity, I wondered? Will I have enough strength to journey the trail?

In this chapter, however hard and emotionally draining it is to put all the accounts into writing, I will share with you how my light was silenced from this side of eternity and transitioned to where she forever shines brightly. I will take you through a series of events that are heartbreaking, without attempting to portray the message as a guide to apply to everyone's circumstances. At the same time, I am hoping to inspire you, and especially those who might be going through similar experiences and wondering if there will be a place for laughter in their hearts again. Trust me, each season has its appointed time, and as we navigate through them all, life grows bigger to ease the weight of the pain endured. I strongly believe in peace that stems from the invisible hand that carries us through our hurting and helps us endure unexplainable pain that we could not otherwise endure. How do you survive the loss of a mother, wife, love, confidant, life partner, etc., and still find strength to live? Only through the personified peace. Peace is real.

November 7th – Graduation

The so long-awaited day had finally arrived. The hope that once seemed unreal was in our reach. The graduation was announced. By the grace and goodness of God, it was a graduation with no student loan; the degree was paid in full. The excitement and gratitude for the day was palpable. We could see the goodness of God at work in our family's life. We were just a few weeks away from the day to celebrate.

Princess's class was initially scheduled to graduate on November 26th, 2018; but for some reason, which to this day I still don't understand, the college suddenly changed the graduation day to November 7th. It came as a surprise but, at the same time, it still felt good as the celebration came closer. I came to understand why the school changed the graduation after the event that followed post November 8th. If you do not believe in a creator of our lives orchestrating every bit of it, I do strongly, beyond any reasonable doubt, believe that he does. I believe and I know for a fact that the date was changed just for Princess to graduate and finish her earthly journey well and fulfilled. Her joy had to be complete before she transitioned.

I was working from home that Wednesday, and the event was to start around 1 p.m. eastern time. I woke up early, prepared the babies to go to school, and let Princess rest. It was her day, so she had all the right to relax and not do much. I started my workday downstairs in our home office until the time came to drive to the school where we would have the event. Just the two of us went because we wanted to have that moment for just the two of us. I vividly recall all we talked about on our way to and from school that day.

I remember how that very night, after graduation, we came home and gathered with our two daughters, my young brother, and my younger sister-in-law to celebrate and thank God for this additional milestone Princess had achieved for her and for our family. We had fun, we ate, and then we took time to express our gratitude. Princess's turn came, and she started by saying: "I am very happy and fulfilled. I have achieved all I had prayed and asked God for. I am happily married, I have given birth to two beautiful daughters, I have just graduated, I have a job, and I am well and healthy." And then she concluded by saying: "I have nothing left to ask God for. Now I will only thank him."

I did not know that she was literarily saying that she had finished her race in this life. It was the first time I had heard Princess making such strong statements, but in that very moment, they did not sound as they were meant to. She meant every word in those two sentences, and in less than 24 hours, she was about to enter another realm.

"Pay attention to the speaking of those you love. That last conversation could actually be the last. Heed them dearly; they will be the force that helps you navigate their physical absence."

We all took our turns; we congratulated her and then said our gratitude to God.

Around 8 p.m., the babies went to bed as the celebration continued for a while. Around 9 p.m., we all went to bed, and the next day we were all working and going to school. I remember we took time to talk in our room about life. Princess asked me a question that troubled me before I could even respond to it. She asked me what I would do if she were to transition. The question caught me off guard as there was nothing that had happened that would possibly have triggered the question. I questioned why she would even ask me that; to my surprise, she insisted that I answer her. Before answering, I asked if she was planning to go. She looked at me and said, "Can you answer my question, please?" I really did not have a proper answer to that. I said, "There is nothing I would do since you are here with me."

We then talked about our end of the year vacation and planned when we would schedule our time off at work to travel with the kids. Then Princess said, "By the way, we need to plan our weekend away without the girls. I really want that to happen sooner than later," she said. We agreed that over the weekend, we were going to look for a venue and book our weekend away.

We revisited our journey from the day we met; we recounted the many blessings we were enjoying after so many setbacks. At the end, she held my hand and said another prayer and then we rested for the night as every other night. Only this one was the final night as a family of four.

Strange Sensation

On October 24, 2018, we had celebrated our 9th wedding anniversary. This was a big step as a couple—only one year remaining to reach the diamond milestone. We had already started planning how the tenth would be celebrated; we would renew our vows.

I was working on a project with one of our financial institution clients in Toronto, and I had visited the client on site that day. Princess had the day off, so during lunch hour, she came to see me, and we went for lunch together, just the two of us. We had booked a restaurant for the evening, to celebrate with family later in the evening.

Something strange happened after we finished our lunch. We stood and started taking pictures and selfies, and as I was taking a picture of her, a strange sensation came over me—a thought flashed through my mind and I saw a picture. I saw Princess transition; she was not alive. I got goosebumps and felt very uncomfortable. She noticed that my face had changed, and she asked what was going on in my mind, but I brushed it off and continued.

After we departed and I went back to the office, I could not stop thinking of what had just happened to me. When I got home, I told Princess what had happened to me. At this point, I believe you know that we had an open communication; we talked about it, but she was using it as an opportunity to tease me on how much I loved her. She made fun of me that I am so much in love that she didn't know how I could live without her, which was entirely true. After the fun part, we prayed about it and asked God to give us peace. She assured me that nothing was going on, and she was not planning to die anytime soon.

This thought, however, bothered me for some time. I wondered why I would feel the way I had felt, especially on our wedding anniversary. It really disturbed me from within even though there was nothing concrete that indicated that it would indeed happen in less than a month. So, when she asked me that question—what I would do if she was not here anymore—on the night of November 7, 2018, the scene of that flash was revived.

I am not sure if these events and many others that I did not capture in this account prepared my inner self for what was going to happen, which would alter the trajectory of my life for the rest of it. When I think about everything that happened—the words that were exchanged, the event that took place, the remarks that Princess would give, how the babies had started relating to us in a different way, etc.—it makes me strongly believe that our souls knew that we were about to be apart.

To give another example of what happened a week before, which was on Thursday, precisely one week before Princess transitioned, I went to pick her up from the office after work. As we drove up Don Valley Parkway from Toronto downtown towards North York, she said that she wanted to call the bank to check a strange transaction she had noticed on her credit card. We dialed the number in the car—we had a joint account so either of us could authenticate with the bank. To our surprise, the bank had wrongly debited six hundred dollars. The agent on the other side of the line apologized and immediately corrected the wrongly debited amount.

What this example taught me is the power of transparency in marriage. Had she not listened to her intuitions about that transaction, or had she not been open with me about it so that we could, together, take the action to check with the bank, the chances were that I would have had a hard time settling that with the bank. It also taught me the meaning of life well lived. She did not leave us with additional financial stress; instead, she cleared everything before she ended her journey with us.

November 8th – Eternal Graduation

We had a routine to wake up and meet with the kids in the living room at 6 a.m. to pray together before departing for the day. I was working from home, so everyone else would leave—Princess going to work and the kids going to school and daycare, and I would also start my workday after I dropped them off.

On this morning, however, something felt strange, but I did not know what it was exactly. The alarm went off, but for some unexplainable reason, I could not wake up. I simply felt I had very low energy and I could not lift my head off my pillow. I was not asleep, but I still failed to wake up. So, I stayed in bed.

Princess did not bother forcing me to join them in the living room; she woke up, greeted me as we would normally do in morning, and then headed to the living room to pray with the babies. I could hear Princess and babies praying loudly in the living room. They prayed for half an hour and then started preparing to leave. After they had breakfast, she came back with the babies to our room and kissed me goodbye for the day. I could not get out of bed. I stayed in bed till around 9 a.m., and then I started work. I really felt very low energy and almost called in to take a sick day, but I shook off the heavy weight I felt and went downstairs to my office.

As it was our custom, when she reached the office, she sent me a text message letting me know that she had arrived well. In the message, she wished me a productive day and reminded me how much she loves me. I responded with the same wishes, and then we were set for the day. We continued checking on each other, as every other day, during the course of the day.

At midday, she called me during her lunch break. Strangely enough, this time she called me on a regular call, which was never the case. We always called on FaceTime unless we were in places where it was not possible to video call. She was comfortably eating, and she was alone and could have called on FaceTime. What surprised me later was that it did not bother me, and I did not even question why we were not using a video call. We talked for a few minutes and then said bye, with the promise to see each other in a few hours. We ended our call with "I LOVE YOU." These were our final words to each other.

I still wonder how she looked as we talked on the phone without looking at each other. Had she been transfigured already? Why didn't I switch on the video call for one more time as she told me how much she loved me? This very call was out of the ordinary, to the point that even the actions changed their normal course. No wonder the following hours darkened. No wonder the breath became heavy like stone. No wonder the light dimmed whilst the sun and stars shone. No wonder even the moon turned its face against me. The end of a chapter was near. Life's single passenger transit system had stopped at my home and did not want to leave without a passenger. Heaven had decided to disrupt my life for a lifetime.

We later texted to check in, but we never spoke again—"I LOVE YOU"; "I LOVE YOU, TOO."

November 8th – 3:53 P.M.

At 3:53 p.m., I received a call from my wife's colleague, announcing that she had been rushed to the hospital in an ambulance after her heart arrested. When the call came in, I did not know the number, but something told me that the call was not going to tell me any good news. I just sensed in my soul that something had happened to Princess. I picked up the call, and the person on the other end of the line inquired if I was Willy, the husband to Estelle. I responded by asking if she was okay. Her voice was shaky and unsure as she informed me that my wife was battling to keep her breath. Then she added, "We called the paramedical who tried to resuscitate her, but her heart was barely beating."

The unexpected had visited my family. The one thing no one would like to hear had just entered my ears with a heavy sound like rushing water. I had been hit at the core.

When I received the call, I was still in my home office, so I turned off my work computer, immediately went downstairs to the garage, and drove to pick up Shayna from the daycare. Kayla was home with her auntie (my sister-in-law), who had just arrived two months before for studies and was staying with us. I dropped Shayna off at home and told them that I was rushing downtown to see their mother. My sister-in-law asked me if her sister was in trouble; I told her that I would know more details once I got there, and I assured her that nothing would happen. "Stay with the babies, have dinner, and go to sleep on time if we take too long to get back home.

I also called my younger brother, who had just moved to Toronto from Edmonton and was staying with us while he searched for his own place. I told him to come home to stay with the kids. He asked where I was going, and I told him the same: "I am going downtown to see Estelle, and I will know more details once I get there."

After I hung up the phone with Estelle's supervisor, I said a simple prayer; I don't think I was conscious of what I said. "God give me peace, guard my heart." That's all I said. On my way to downtown, I was calm. I did not speed, and I did not know what to think. What I remember is that I felt peace in my heart that I cannot explain in the lines of this book. I played a song called "You Made a Way," by Travis Greene. The song was on repeat for the time I was on the highway, from our home to the hospital.

A thought came into my heart to call my mother and my mother-in-law. I called both of them to let them know what was happening. I requested them to pray for us. My mother-in-law, whom I loved so dearly and she loved me so much, told me to stay strong, whatever the outcome would be. She later on told me that she had sensed that her dear daughter was going home. What hurt her most was that she went before her. She had wished to transition before her, but heaven decided otherwise.

HOSPITAL – I arrived at the hospital after half an hour or so. When I entered the reception area, I told them that I was there to see my wife, who had been brought in by an ambulance. They verified my identification and then escorted me to the ICU area. This was my first time being in an intensive care area; medical staff were running from one side to another. There, I saw my wife's colleague, who had come with her, and her cardiologist had arrived. He knew me, so he immediately walked towards me.

I was so calm and peaceful in my heart, but when I saw his facial expression, I knew things were not right. Nevertheless, in the back of my mind, something told me that Princess was well. We shook hands and then I asked, "How is my wife?" He immediately told me that things were not looking good. "Medically speaking, I am not confident your wife will survive," he said.

I melted within, yet I still felt peaceful. At this time, I had not been able to see my wife yet. She was with a specialist, who was doing what they could to save her life. After 15 minutes or so, I asked to see my wife. It just felt wrong not to be with her and speak to her, regardless of the state she was in. I knew she would hear me even if she did not respond to me.

The cardiologist went in to ask if they could allow me to come in. A minute after, he walked out and called me to go in. I stood up but I could not feel my body. Remember the two questions I was asked in my car? The same voice came back again: "If this is the last time you are going to see Estelle alive, what will you do and what will you say? How about the dreams and plans you share? Will they be silenced with her?" This conversation happened as I walked into the intensive care room my princess was being treated in. I again responded with the same thing. I will tell you my responses below.

I entered the room and saw my light lying on the hospital bed with life support devices attached to her. I still felt peace within, but my body simply would not take it in. I literally melted from within, and I felt confused and powerless. What struck me most was that my wife was surrounded by 8 medical staff; there were machines everywhere, but when I looked at her, it was as if she was just sleeping. Had she not been in the hospital with all that was going on, she just looked the way she looked when she slept. This contrast troubled me. I saw the urgency that was on these doctors' faces, and they were talking non-stop in their medical terms, but when I looked at my princess, the two images did not correlate. I wondered how one could be in critical condition and still not reflect the pain. My light was dimming.

Touch with No Response

I approached the bed and reached out to hold her hand, and for the very first time, she did not react to my touch. I was lost. It had been 14 years since we had met, and 9 years of marriage, and there had been no single day that my light had not responded to my touch—never. How could she just not react, I wondered? When I came in, somehow, I hoped that she would open her eyes and look at me. I hoped that when I touched her, I would see tears flow down her cheeks, and I would wipe them. I was hoping to look in her eyes and tell her that I was there and that we were in this together.

Nothing of the above happened. I leaned towards her and kissed her forehead, still hoping that she would make eye contact, but nothing happened. I was so troubled from within. No one else in that room expressed the same pain. Yes, the medical staff were doing their job. However, I missed having someone I could hold tight in order to exhale.

My breath felt so heavy, and my heart was heavy, like a stone in my chest. I failed to cry.

The life supporting devices indicated that she was still alive, but she was in a deep unconscious state. The room was full of specialists doing all they could do to bring her back, but it was too late; their laudable efforts were in vain.

In the next minute or so, the main doctor asked me to sit outside of the room; they were going to shock her with electricity to try and resuscitate her. Another medical staff accompanied me and sat me on a chair and requested that I lie down. He then said, "Please take this juice to increase your sugar level. You might be short of oxygen as your brain is under shock." I don't think I tasted anything, but I took the drink anyway.

We were at the hospital for over four hours. Then the lead medical doctor came out of the room and told me: "Your wife will be gone in exactly 15 minutes. Please come and say goodbye to her."

I screamed and begged him to do whatever was in his power to bring my wife back. He calmly told me, "Sir, I have done all I could; at this stage, all vital organs have failed. Your wife's heart will completely stop in no more than 15 minutes. Please go and say your goodbyes." I stood up and walked into the room. Somehow, I still hoped that Princess would wake up. She had never done this before; never had she ever given up on me—why would she do it now, when we are on the mountaintop of our life? I strongly believed she was just sleeping because she looked as beautiful as the first day I saw her, and she lay so peacefully.

Facing Death

As I entered the room, to my surprise, everyone was leaving; it suddenly became quiet. All medical staff left and went back to their duties. I felt so lonely. I felt abandoned. I felt completely lost. It was now just me, facing death. How do you explain that in less than a minute, a room filled with people just emptied as if no one cared? Did they really understand what I was going through, I questioned? Why not even stay to comfort me?

I was not able to cry. I was numb. Yet, I felt peace. I looked at my wife, the only individual who knew me inside out; the person with whom I shared everything and nothing, lying there unresponsive. I talked to her in the hope that she would at least nod or say goodbye, but I did not hear her voice again, nor did I feel her response to my touch. I asked her, "Princess, can you tell me what to tell Kayla and Shayna?" For the first time, she was lying down and seemed to ignore my inquiry. I will spare you my last words to her. I felt disarmed, I felt lost, I felt confused. I lay next to her; I held her beautiful, soft hands, and then I kissed her goodbye. I remember our cardiologist coming in and looking confused. He consoled me and questioned why Estelle was gone. It was my first time seeing a medical specialist cry over his patient.

He had seen her a few weeks back when he did all the tests and told her the good news that she was healed of the deficiency that had been diagnosed a few years before. "How could this happen? I did not see this coming," he said. Then he hugged me and left.

My wife was gone. I felt angry at myself for not being able to save her life as I had always done. I had treasured, provided, protected, loved, and cherished her wholeheartedly. How could I fail her when she needed me most, I asked myself! For the very first time, I lost the battle for the love of my life. I was faced with reality, death, and human limitation.

The world had become so small in my sight that I did not find a room to run to. The strength of my youth was cut short and my vitality incapacitated. Where had the young man gone, who could do all in his power to rescue his love? How do you explain this loss? I was not even given an opportunity to fight before the referee whistled the final score. I felt unfairly judged; the verdict was partial. When it's all said and done, our riches and connections become powerless; only the small light inside is what carries us through.

"When it's all said and done, what matters is the light we carry inside, the love we truly cherish and the memory we treasure."

I was lonely. I was numb. I could not leave the room, yet the medical staff needed to proceed with their process. As I walked outside the room, into the hallway to the lift, and then outside of the hospital, I felt the weight of the pain and the state of being incapacitated. I could not recognize where I had parked my car, so my brother and Princess's colleagues, who were there, searched for a few minutes. Fortunately, my brother was there to drive me back home.

Announcing the News to Our Daughters

I got home around midnight, and as soon as I entered the house, my sister-in-law asked me where her sister was. I had no words. I just nodded my head and said I was sorry. You can imagine what followed. Babies woke up from their sleep. I held both of them, and we entered into my room and did not say much. They asked me what had happened. "Dad, where is Mum? What happened? Why are auntie and uncle crying? Why are these people here?" The news had gone ahead of us and people had started coming home to comfort. I am still so grateful to be part of a community that cares.

How do you explain to a 7-year-old and a 2-year-old that their mother is gone and won't be returning? How do you explain death to them? My response was that Mum was not coming back. "Why," they both asked. Mum went to heaven; she won't come back, but one day we will go there, and we will see her." I held them tight until they fell asleep again. The solitary journey had just started.

Princess's Homecoming

The next day, I had to decide what the process was going to be. We were new in Canada and the majority of our family was in Rwanda. My mother-in-law, at that time, was not able to travel, so I had to decide quickly on where I would have my wife laid to rest. I thought about it and could not see how I would be at peace knowing that my mother-in-law was not able to say goodbye to her daughter. So, I decided that we would travel with Princess to Rwanda for final ceremonies and funerals. I had no idea what this decision implied, but that was the least I could do in my remaining power.

I will not go into the details of what followed—arranging funeral ceremonies and traveling to Rwanda for Princess's homecoming. However, it is worth mentioning the power of love. I understood the power of love that is beyond that of death. I loved Estelle so powerfully that I did not have the right to give in to the unbearable sorrow of losing my soulmate. I realized that it would be a dishonor to her legacy, to my beliefs, to our two gorgeous daughters, and to the life that I still live, to be overtaken by despair during her passing. It was and still is painful to ever revisit the experience. Even the thought of it gives me goosebumps; nevertheless, there was so much that expected me to stay strong and carry on. Life does not pause as we hurt; it does not give us a break to process before we can proceed. The life pace continues its course.

I prayed to God to show me his mercies even amidst the shadow of death that I and our babies were going through. Boy, God did come through. He provided me with peace and inner calmness that I could not understand nor explain. People from across the globe, the majority of whom I did not know, stood up to help in all ways you can possibly think of. The support we received globally made the weight somehow lighter, and we were able to organize a homecoming ceremony for Princess in Kigali, Rwanda, in the presence of our families.

It is a terrible thing to lose your spouse, but it is unexplainably difficult to lose your spouse far from your families and in a new country with limited connections. I was deeply concerned about my mother-in-law. She was very close and an intimate friend to her daughter. At that time, she was unable to travel, and I was unable to lay my wife to rest without my mother-in-law. She would not have survived the shock. I called her and told her that I had decided to have all ceremonies and the funeral in Kigali, where she lived.

Having been able to allow my mother-in-law to say goodbye to her dearest daughter was a steppingstone towards the healing journey. It was extremely hard to arrange all the logistics for international travel in such circumstances; it was so emotionally draining; but being able to honor my light traditionally, surrounded by family and those who knew us well, did ease the pain to some degree.

I take this opportunity to thank those near and far who have thought of us, prayed for us, and contributed in one way or another to make the process possible. Your love was felt so much amidst the unspeakable loss.

During the three weeks of organizing and traveling, I asked myself so many important questions. One of them was, if God and life had come to me and said, "We have a mission to take you or your wife. But before we do so, we want to give you a chance to make a choice, and we will go with what you choose." I wondered, if that scenario had occurred, what my response would have been.

My answer was at my fingertips: Without hesitation, I would have chosen my princess to go first. Why? There are two main reasons: One, because the pain and void of losing your other half is too heavy, and I would not wish, even for a second, for my princess to experience it. The second reason is because I knew that if heaven exists, which I strongly believe is the case, my princess would be in a better place. There is no possible logical explanation that would convince me that purehearted people like Estelle, would die and that is the end of it. There is a better place they go to.

"If God would have given me the option, I would still choose the same, because the pain and void of losing your love is so deep that I would not rest in peace knowing that Princess was left behind with such a void."

Till Death Do Us Part

During the two weeks we had to organize the travel to Rwanda, to get the proper documentation and flight itinerary, I took time to think about what was happening. Yes, I was still in a complete denial phase. I looked at our wedding rings; I revisited our plans and dreams. I ruminated on our life journey and all the conversations we'd had for all those years, especially the last two years. Something dawned on my spirit. I was brought to the saying, "Till death do us part."

I meditated on what these five words meant. Did they mean that I was departing from Estelle for good? Did they mean that love stops when your spouse dies? What do they really mean? As I continued to think about those words, I realized that my vows to Estelle had attained their validity date—the vows to stay together, the vows to provide and protect, the vows to faithfully nurture and support, the vows to cling to and journey the trail of life through highs and lows, the vows… They had all reached their validity date.

I struggled very much to accept these facts. This reality seemed to suggest that my love for her was also reaching its validity date, which was and still is not the case. The vows we made to each other had reached their maturity date; however, the love remains, and it is the force that sustained me through the unbearable pain of grief. It is the love reflected in the memories created together, and the impacts made in each other's life that carries us through. Because of the journey taken in perfect harmony, that love enables the survivor to honor and carry the torch until it is passed on to the next in line.

In the midst of what was happening, I still found time, when everyone was asleep, to process my thoughts. I came to terms with my heart and accepted that all the vows I had with Princess had matured at the validity date that had come unannounced. Even though this was true, it did not mean, in any way, that my love for her would ever mature; its validity is eternal.

So, to signify what I had realized—les faits sont têtues: "Facts are stubborn"—I resolved to take off my wedding ring. I took my ring, her two other rings—the engagement ring and the wedding ring—and I read the Bible scripture we had on our wedding invitation card: Psalm 23, verse 6.

"Surely your goodness and love (mercy) will follow me all the days of my life, and I will dwell in the house of the Lord forever."

The last day, in a room at the hospital in Kigali, as I was saying my last goodbyes, I took all three rings and put them on Princess's lifeless fingers. I was numb; the pain was so deep that my tears dried up. My last words were, as I did that act: "I cannot wait to see you on the other side of eternity." I let my light go because heaven had decided to interrupt.

At that particular moment, I realized how small and short our lives are compared to eternity. I wished I could redeem the time I had wasted in small fights. I wished I could get time back to support my princess in every little endeavor she undertook. I wished I had spent more time with her, more weekends away, more travels, etc. Everything else ceased to matter in the face of the eternal life perspective.

My Farewell

Dear families and friends gathered here today, allow me to thank you all for your support and empathy shown during this long journey that my daughters and I have started after our princess and queen transitioned to the other side of eternity.

I assure you, I won't take much of your time as I don't have much to say. One thing I would like to mention, however, is that despite the grief and sorrow that are deeper than words can express, I am here to celebrate my princess's life well lived on this side of eternity.

I, therefore, would like to invite you all, especially my family and my family-in-law and closest friends, to celebrate with us in spite of the pain and separation.

My key notes today will focus on what I think Princess would have wanted me to say. If I start talking about her, my life with her, I assure you that we will need at least a few days to cover just a small part.

Life is like a book with many chapters. Some have books with 70 chapters; some have more, and some less. To each chapter, God has assigned 365 pages. The size of our books does not really matter, at least not to God; the size does not weigh much. What counts is that we have all been given pens to write what we want others to read from our books. Sometimes we write well, by our choices and actions. Other times, we do not do well. Regardless of what you and I have written in the current chapter, a new chapter beckons.

As we celebrate my princess's life, I can tell you, beyond any reasonable doubt, that she has written well all her 36 chapters, especially the last one.

I am confident that she is resting in heaven.

I am here today, as we celebrate her life, to remind you and myself to do all we can to make sure that we make the new chapter we have been given count. Why? Because we do not know if this is the last chapter or not. The last chapter and last page of your life's book determine whether or not your name is in God's book of life. They are the entry door to your next life beyond sight.

The going home of my princess has not only left me heartbroken as a husband and a father, but it has also taught me about God's love and heaven.

In his sovereign love, God puts his own interest first. After all, we humans do the same too. We do all it takes to get to where we want, and to obtain the best we can in our power.

In his sovereign love, God shows no favoritism. He does what he wants on his own terms and in his own way.

In our cultures, most of us here, when choosing a bride or who to marry, you study the character of the bride but also that of her family. Who does not want to marry a beautiful—inside and out—bride? Who does not want to marry someone from a rich and well-known family with a good reputation?

This painful experience taught me to thank my Lord, in spite of the grief and unspeakable pain. It has also given me assurance and comfort that one day I will see her—who does not want to visit her daughter when she is married to a rich, handsome son-in-law?

Heaven is real. If it wasn't the case, Princess would not have gone. She was so ready, so happy, and wished to meet her savior.

I feared God. I received so much reverence to God because he dared me, and his love won over mine. With the love and commitment I had with my princess and our gorgeous daughters, only God could break it. He did not care (humanly speaking) that my earthly father had passed on when I was only 2 years old. He did not care (humanly speaking) that we had so many plans for each other and for our daughters. No, he loved her more than all of us. The book's chapters assigned to her were well written and it was time to call her home.

God provides peace and comfort through it all. I must say that God has given us peace and comfort that we cannot understand. How can you explain that we continue living when Princess is no longer with us?

God knows it best. I have come to understand that only God understands and knows everything. The only option left for me is to choose to put my trust in him and live to write my chapters well. He knows me better than I know myself. He also knows the two little princesses he has entrusted me with. He cares, even though it may seem like he does not.

I now live with something to look forward to. I strive to live a life with a heavenly perspective. I cannot wait to meet Princess, with the Lord, across the river. This is the biggest challenge Princess and her going home left me with.

In conclusion, I want to thank you all, once again, for the love and support you have shown us. We will never be able to thank you enough!

These were my final words as we sent my princess to her eternal resting place. Re-typing these words revives all the emotions and, at the same time, it awakens all senses of gratitude to God for seeing us through. Looking back, five years from the day I spoke these words, it is so true and beneficial to choose to live, even after losing your most treasurable person, while trusting God for his guidance.

God's Will – A Bitter Pill to Swallow

I am a strong believer of the gospel of Jesus of love, a pure love that is not absent of suffering. Nevertheless, I struggled so much, and I still do struggle, to understand God's will in our lives, as it does not always align with our logical thought process. Logically, if you love someone, like I loved Estelle and how much I love Kayla and Shayna, the last thing you would want is to allow any suffering to come their way, especially if you have control over the circumstances that may trigger the suffering.

I have done and will still do till my last breath, all that is in my power to protect them and ensure that nothing in my control can cause any life disruptive event in their lives.

When it comes to the love of God, however, we see the contrary happen. Yet, I know that he loves me so much, and I also know that he is all powerful and can prevent any hurt from reaching me. Why does he still let me suffer? What is his will for me? I wondered to the point that I started questioning my faith in God.

In my quest to understand what life is and what God's will for my life is, I realized how much he actually loves me. Yes, he knows that life sucks, and suffering will be inevitable. Although he does not approve of it, he knows very well that it will happen that we will cry and hurt, so he chooses to stay with us to help us navigate through it.

It is like a parent with his children. I have two of them that I love more than I can ever express. Even though I know that when they go out to school, they might get hurt—fall down and twist their ankles, be bullied, etc.—I still let them go. I see them playing in dirt; I see them eating without properly washing their hands, and I know they could catch bacteria and viruses, etc. Do I prevent them from trying things out? No, but I still see them and help when they fall. Does it mean that I love them less? Absolutely not.

I came to understand that life will have many setbacks, including death, but that does not mean that God's will for me is evil, nor is it any less loving. He continues to sustain even when I do not feel that way, and that makes his will a very bitter pill to swallow.

In the next chapter, I will discuss how I navigated the loss of my dear wife. I purposely called this phase "honoring my light." I could have used grieving, but to me it makes more sense to honor, because grief connotates mainly the negative aspect of the process. Yes, it is a grieving journey with a sense of honoring and intentionally choosing to do so in order to navigate the grief. Thank you for staying with me this far. In the remainder of this book, I will strive to encourage you, to inspire you, and to remind you that even after the light fades aways, there is a hope that remains to dare to live again.

"I believe that imagination is stronger than knowledge. That myth is more potent than history. That dreams are more powerful than facts. That hope always triumphs over experience. That laughter is the only cure for grief. And I believe that love is stronger than death."
~Robert Fulghum~

"Grief is the price we pay for love."
~Queen Elizabeth II~

Chapter 7

Life Without My Light Is Possible
Because Hope Remains

L ife is an open-ended school journey. Every step of the way is a new step we need to adapt to. But where do you start from when you just lost your spouse at a very young age, and when life seems to be in its glorious phase? Where do you start in explaining to a seven-year-old and a two-year-old that their mother, who had left for work in the morning, would not be returning for good? How do you wrap your mind around the realization of living a life of widowhood, with parenting responsibilities, career responsibilities, social duties, and the calling of your life? What do you drop for the benefit of doing better for the others? There are valid reasons not to give up, but how do you do that and where do you start?

These are all valid and reasonable questions that I, and most probably many others, have had to face in one way or another. So, my discussion in these pages might be different from others you might have read or experienced. I am not proposing a manual on how to answer them and live a life after a life altering event, but rather a personal life experience account with the hope of inspiring you on how to navigate your specific setback.

I lost my wife when I was 38 years of age. At that point, I had lived in five countries across three continents. I interacted and mingled with different people from different backgrounds and cultures. I had experienced loss, rejection, and hardship, right from my childhood experiences of being raised and brought up in a lawless country, to becoming a teenager and adolescent in a country that had just gone through the last human tragedy of the twentieth century—the genocide against Tutsi in Rwanda. I matured while on a refugee journey in the West; then I achieved my highest potential—marriage and family, and education and career—in the two hemispheres of the Western world, Europe and North America.

Nothing of the aforementioned experiences had prepared me on how to live after losing the other half of myself. My master's degree did not provide me with the tools on how to handle and survive loss. My successful career did not equip me with any helpful tool; on the contrary, it demanded all of my attention in order to excel and keep providing. Even my beliefs and faith did not prepare me on how to manage the natural pain and suffering that derive from losing your life companion.

We had only been in Canada for two years, and the majority of our close friends and those who knew us well were in Europe. I am naturally a social person; when I arrive in a new environment, I try to build new relationships and build new connections. Canada was no different; as hard as it is to make new friends, I had managed to make substantial and meaningful connections with people in different communities from the Great Lakes Region of Africa: Uganda, Burundi, Rwanda, and Congo. We had also been part of the Church on the Queensway (still my church to date), and there were also co-workers, colleagues, and clients. There I was, surrounded by family and friends, yet lonely and trying to face reality.

I still do not comprehend how everyone was compelled to come out and support me and my family through the hard time we were going through. I recall that from the few hours that followed the passing on of

Princess, our house was full of people, the majority of whom I did not know and who did not know Estelle at all. The next day, we had to find a big hall to host everyone for the two weeks that followed. Seeing so many people come out to comfort was an act of love in action that I witnessed.

At this time, I was still numb. My thought process was still in the denial phase. Yes, my wife was no longer with us, but my life had not yet comprehended it. The two questions the invisible voice had posed to me as I drove downtown were still loud and clear in my heart. I had been very vocal about it during the ceremonies, and I could not wait any longer. I had choices to make. I had lives that depended on my response for their survival. My two fragile, gorgeous daughters' hope for living solely depended on my response to the loss of their mother and the actions thereof. My family's tranquility heavily depended on my attitude and well-being. Would he make it? they wondered. My close friends and inner circle worried much and doubted, to some extent, my ability to make it without Princess by my side. After all, I was just a young man with no experience on how to run a household and all other obligations, combined with grieving my loved one.

I had choices to make, and only I could make those choices. No one, however much everyone cared and was concerned, could help carry the weight and make things move forward. There were two possible and probable options: either to break completely or to hope and move forward despite the unbearable pain. I intentionally chose to work towards my healing, on my own terms, and started the journey immediately. The pain was so much that doing nothing would have been a waste altogether.

*"The pain of losing Princess was too much to waste.
It would be a dishonor to her life, to God, and to myself
to give into despair and lose hope for life."*

Returning from Kigali

During the mourning period while in Toronto, and the two weeks we spent in Kigali for funeral ceremonies, we were surrounded by family and friends. I did not have time to think about myself and actually reflect on what had just happened to us. The babies were also in the same boat as me, and for them, nothing made sense anyway. In one instance, they would be playing with other kids, and in a moment, their moods would change.

On November 30, 2018, we traveled back to Toronto. From the moment we boarded the plane, the weight of loss fell on me. I realized that what seemed like an unreal dream, had actually happened. I was traveling back with my two girls, without their mother, my soulmate. My body was weak and my soul was downcast, yet I had to make sure the traveling was smooth for the babies and start creating an environment where they would feel safe and secure. We were accompanied by my niece and sister-in-law, which helped a lot during this eighteen-hour trip.

It was on Saturday, December 1, 2018, and on Monday, Kayla and Shayna had to return back to school, and I had to go back to work too. We had spent a few weeks with close to no sleep, and we were jetlagged. I had to start reinstating the habits of sleeping on time for the babies before they returned to school, but I could barely sleep.

Back to School

The hardest part of the journey had just started. I had a school-aged daughter and one in daycare, whose preparations and expectations are quite different. The school-aged daughter was aware, to some extent, of what had happened, but she still could not make sense of it. She was afraid of going back to school because everyone knew that she no longer had a mother. She felt lost and afraid to see her friends; she was not sure how to manage her emotions. The youngest was completely lost; she could not formulate her questions because nothing made sense in her mind. She was fine going to daycare, but because she did not know what was happening within, she would get agitated and just need to be held in my arms for security.

Fortunately, both schools had tools to help children navigate through their emotions. When I took Kayla to school for the first time, we were warmly welcomed by her classmates and teachers, who had made a big paper card with comforting notes on it. They all surrounded her with hugs and made her comfortable. It was so emotional to experience that everyone was in tears. I was asked to stay and see how she would adjust. After a few minutes, Kayla, in her bravery, came and told me, "Dad, you can leave. I am fine. If I need you, my teacher will call you to come back." She just assured me and allowed me to go back. These are moments that would make you proud in normal circumstances, but in this case, it made me feel powerless. It felt like I was leaving my daughter unassisted.

Then I took Shayna to her daycare. I remember when we pulled over in the parking lot; I lifted her from her car seat, and as we worked our way upstairs, she looked at me and asked, "Daddy, why is Mum in heaven? Why did she go without us?" This was a question from a 3-year-old.

I did not know what to answer, and I could not hold back my tears. She then looked at me and said, "It's okay, Daddy. Don't cry." I held her tight, kissed her, and we entered the building. She was also warmly welcomed back with gladness from her teachers and classmates. One thing to note about Shayna, she started speaking when she was around one and half years old. She is very sociable. So, whenever she enters a room, her presence is immediately noticed. Her groupmates had missed her dearly. She kissed me and said, "Bye, Daddy."

My drive back home was one of the hardest in my life. I had just experienced an energy draining event to which I did not know how to respond. I was fortunate that I had been working from home; had it not been the case, I am not sure if I would have made it to the office that particular day. Day one passed, and all seemed to go well despite the heavy emotions involved.

Letting Go of Palpable Reminders

Up until this point, I was still dealing with the side effects of losing my soulmate. I had not found time to face the grief from within and the connection to palpable material that represented my union with Estelle. Being busy with the girls and their school and after-school activities, spending my days working and interacting with colleagues and serving clients, and other daily activities kind of took my attention. In reality, the busyness served as an escape tool. I did not have time to sit down and realize what had just happened, so I took refuge in denial.

Nothing had changed just yet in the house. Everything in the house was still the same, including wardrobes. In my room, the decorations and all that you would find in a couple's room were still intact. I still sensed and felt Estelle's physical presence. It was as if she had just traveled for business or vacation, and she would return. Somehow, the house configuration helped and emphasized the denial state. All her clothes and other possessions were there. The difference was just that she had left, but it felt like she would return soon.

Around Christmas time, December 23, 2018, I had to make another decision to let go. I personally took time to take every item, one by one, and pack them in a big sackcloth and load them into the car to take them to the donation center. I selected a few souvenirs that I deemed important to keep for the girls, but everything that had to be donated, I took the painful decision to do it myself.

That was the day I first cried and wept for my wife. I had not had the occasion to pour out my heart and let the emotions be expressed. Taking each item one by one felt like part of my life was being taken from me. It took me half a day to let go of the things that were in our room. However hard and painful it was during those hours, after I deposited them at the donation center and returned home, I felt lighter than I was before doing it. This was the first step to the realization of Princess's absence in my life.

After letting go of the material things, I felt the total absence of the one I had loved and shared treasurable memories of my life with. The house felt completely empty, especially since I was working from home while Kayla and Shayna were at school. I had to face the blunt reality of widowhood. I started journaling (I will share some letters I would send to Princess, in the section below). I lost my appetite for almost everything, including phone calls. I entertained only necessary calls because of responsibilities.

Household Management

In our marriage, Princess and I did everything together. However, we had clear roles and responsibilities. Unless I was sick or not home, Princess would not do the cleaning in the house alone. It was my responsibility to do the vacuuming, take out the garbage, lift heavy stuff, and fix things in the house. She would, of course, help, but these were my responsibilities. I would also bathe the babies to give her time to prepare as well, and then she would do their hair and all the other final touches.

On the other hand, cooking (I only cooked on the weekend), shopping for groceries and clothes, budgeting household expenditures, planning visits and vacations, doing homework with the babies, and making sure I was doing what I was supposed to do, just to name a few, were her responsibilities.

We, 80% of the time, did all tasks together, but as a man, my attention span was limited. I had to be reminded over and over again where to find things. I would look for a shirt in the wardrobe but not find it, yet it would be right in front of my face.

Now I had to do all household tasks, manage everything, and help the babies navigate the grief process, as I continued to provide a secure and safe environment. I had to learn how to organize the babies' wardrobes and make daily decisions on what they should wear, what they should eat for breakfast, what they should pack for school, and what would be for dinner, Monday to Sunday. I had to learn how to cook the variety of meals that Princess would make (she was one of the best when it came to creative cooking). I had to know where in the shop to buy groceries and required ingredients/recipes to make healthy meals. I would pray and ask God to guide and lead me to the things I knew Estelle would do. Many times, I would go to the grocery store and pray to find a particular item; and trust me when I say this: It would go as I prayed. When I would be cooking, I would just pray to God to help me make the meal just as she had made it; to my surprise, the meal would turn out to be more or less the same. How do I know, you might ask? Kayla would give me a compliment by saying, "Dad, your food tastes exactly like Mama's." It hurt but also helped me to feel that the babies were still getting what they were accustomed to.

Not Me But Them

As I navigated through the process of learning how to live and do things by myself, I did not see the need for, or the importance of, including myself among those who needed rest and time to grieve. I did not have time to think about my well-being; all that mattered was to make sure the babies were well taken care of, the work was done, and I could still deliver. My state did not seem to matter much to me. I guess I did not see how detrimental not taking care of yourself could be.

I had lost weight and my appetite, and the course continued to be the same. I was losing my energy, and my body was very weak. I did not have any alternative and my personality accentuated it. I am a hardworking person and do not complain or show my emotions easily. My family and friends could notice the weight loss but did not see me slowing down, and they did not know how to make me realize that.

My mindset is programed in a way that, if there is something that needs to be done and it's in my ability to do it, I hardly leave a task unfinished. So, I continued on the same path of not resting but working hard; I kept doing me. At some point, my niece and sister-in-law confronted me and asked me to slow down. Then my brother and other friends told me the same thing; but me being me, I did not really see that I was doing beyond what I was supposed to do. Yes, my body was weak, but I was not sick, and things had to be done. I had to make sure everyone was taken care of.

My life journey had shaped me to work hard, take responsibly, and hold myself accountable to everything I do. This is a character I developed at young age. I also started setting my standards at a very high bar. I don't leave things undone, nor do I complain when things go opposite to my expectations. When Princess passed, I became harder on myself. I felt that I did not have room left for error or underdelivering. In addition, I felt that my daughters needed to have me 200%, as their father, their mother, and everything in between. I felt that I needed and was required to maintain a certain level of life standard without putting any sort of excuses in front of me.

As time passed by, I felt weak physically; however, I did not slow down or show any sign of weakness in my dealing with life in general. Not by my might, but somehow, God sustained me and still is sustaining me to keep the pace.

Avoiding Facing It – Self-Regulating

I eventually realized that in addition to my personality, I was also taking refuge in my busyness. Having all my hours filled with tasks to accomplish did not leave me any room to think and process the loss. I was up early and slept late, so I would be able to catch some sleep, and the circle would restart the next morning. I started reading about suffering and grief as a way to assess myself. I took time to actually allow my emotions to surface; it dawned on me that I was forgetting myself.

I had to face myself and intentionally create room for grief. I resolved to take time every evening, once the babies were asleep, to isolate in the basement and express myself. I vocalized my hurt, let out my deepest emotions, questioned life and God, and expressed my anger and pain that I could not explain to anyone in a logical way. After saying it as I felt it, I would always end with a prayer, asking God for peace and strength. As time passed, each day was better than the previous day.

Through reading, meditation, and intentional-auto-regulated self-awareness, I started creating repeatable routines and processes to follow. I made a schedule of routines to follow on a daily basis. The intention was to be able to say no to some things in order to do others, and at the same time find joy of living as I continued to develop in the new journey I had started.

I started following my routine and made sure I had time for myself to pour out my heart and process my thoughts. Having the benefit of working from home helped me plan my day with much ease.

I have been following the same template since 2018. I am not claiming to be a perfectionist here; I do miss a few steps in my schedule from time to time, but the high-level guidelines did help me process my loss and manage my household and work, while taking care of my well-being. I am still following the same template to date to maximize my productivity, while I efficiently manage my energy level.

Below is high-level schedule of what my normal day schedule looks like. It should be in full page and in color, but it's not. The table gives you an idea of how you can schedule repeatable routines to increase your productivity, while managing your time efficiently. If you want to see the real schedule, download the full-size, full-color, print-ready version at www.WhenLightFadesAwayHopeRemains.com, and adapt it to make it your own.

TIME	MON	TUE	WED	THU	FRI	SAT	SUN
6:00 a.m. - 6.30 a.m.	Quiet time	Quiet time	Quiet time	Quiet time	Quiet time	Quiet time	Quiet time
6.30 a.m. - 7.20 a.m.	Get Ready	Get Ready	Get Ready	Get Ready	Get Ready	Get Ready & Family Time	Get Ready & Family Time
7.20 a.m. –7.30 a.m.	Take kids to school	Take kids to school	Take kids to school	Take kids to school	Take kids to school		
7.30 a.m. – 8:00a.m.	Devotional	Devotional	Devotional	Devotional	Devotional		
8:00 a.m.– 12:00 p.m.	Work	Work	Work	Work	Work	Chores	Church
12:00 a.m. – 1:00 p.m.	Lunch Time	Lunch Time	Lunch Time	Lunch Time	Lunch Time	Lunch Time	Lunch Time
1:00 p.m. – 5:00 p.m.	Work	Work	Work	Work	Work	Family Time	Family Time
5:00 p.m. – 8:00 p.m.	Family Time	Family Time	Family Time	Family Time	Family Time		
8:00 p.m. – 10:00 p.m.	Me time	Me time	Me time	Me time	Me time		
10:00 p.m. -	Bed	Bed	Bed	Bed	???	???	Bed

* I do not do all tasks at the same time. The schedule helps me know when to do what. As an example, for the family time, it's not every day that we do homework. It's not every day that I work on my business, write songs, etc. The time is to facilitate my prioritization and task allocation.

Legend

Quiet time: Wake-up, hydrate, mediating and praying for the day ahead.
Get Ready: Waking up the kids, breakfast, packing lunch box for the babies.
Take kids to school: Kids catch the bus to school.
Devotional: Bible devotional, motivational reading, mindset repurposing.
Work: Meetings, priorities, team building, etc.

Family Time: Homework, playtime, reading with kids, friends, exercise, activities, etc.

Me time: Self- development, personal work, personal prayer time, journaling, writing, and recording song.

The Next Right Thing

It is not straight forward to stay motivated, stay focused, and to keep an eye on the bigger picture to allow yourself to see the end of the tunnel. It can, oftentimes, become extremely difficult to accomplish tasks whilst you keep your thoughts healthy.

Even though I had implemented a routine process to help me organize my days around our family life, each new day brought its own challenges, and the weight of loneliness never seemed to lighten.

Doing the next right thing along the way, however small it might be, was the only way out. I figured that even washing that one spoon after making tea, folding the blanket after watching TV with the babies, making my bed right after waking up, putting away dishes after washing them, etc., was the only way I could make room for the next day's tasks.

It turned out to be efficient for each next day, starting from a place that is empty of any carried over and unfinished work. It became much easier to walk with the babies to the nearby playground each afternoon if the other small chores were complete.

Even though I did not, and still don't, see the way out of this solitary journey, focusing my energy on that next right thing around me helped me cope with my grief and efficiently achieve my daily goals, in my life's context. God, who seemingly had forsaken me, continued to carry me through even in the unseen processes of life.

Reading and Writing Songs

I have always loved to read, especially motivational and leadership development books. It provides me peace and stirs up my motivation to work to improve myself in different areas of my life across different domains. As life expands, we get busier and tend to slow down on things that we once loved doing. Because of traveling and moving to different countries, I was reading less and less. I picked up my reading habit again. This was the only conversation I enjoyed having, in my quiet time, when everything else seemed silent.

I read the Bible, questioned its promises, and wondered if my faith was actually real. I also read about suffering, love, and grief, and many other topics, including money and finances (I am an economist by education and professional). As I continued reading, I did find the joy and peace within. I did not find answers to my many questions; however, I found strength to carry on. The reading habit also triggered other dormant potentials I had ignored for some time. I awakened my song writing talent.

I had started writing songs when I met Princess, and we continued to write songs together. Moving from country to country and expanding my responsibilities kind of played down my song writing talent, which resulted in not recording any of our artwork. As I navigated the journey after her passing, this poetic trait was revived. I revisited songs we had written many years back, and I wrote new ones, which I ended up recording on my very first album. There are still many that I have not yet recorded and are still on the to-do list, both from the old list and the new one that I have been writing as the inspiration comes to me.

These two habits helped me, extremely, to manage and express my emotions in ways I would not have been able to otherwise. I was able to express unspoken words through songs and process my thoughts and feelings through reading. When I look at the statistics of how many people these simple songs have touched across the globe, it gives me joy that my grief cannot take away. It reminds me how big our lives are—we are not limited by the parameters around our current life's circumstances; we are more than that.

Response to Two Questions

The two questions I was asked by the invisible but clear and audible voice in my car as I drove to the hospital on November 8, 2018, remained intense and a constantly resounding voice in my heart. I was grieving and learning to reshape our lives, but in the back on my mind, the two questions were calling for an answer, and without any delay.

For the sake of recapping them, after I received the phone call that my wife had been rushed to the hospital after having cardiac arrest while in the office, I heard a voice asking me what I would do and say, and how I would behave if that very evening was the last time I was to see Estelle alive. The voice continued and asked me what I was going to do with all the plans and dreams we shared. "Are you going to let them to be silenced with her?" the voice had asked.

I later on realized that this conversation was preparing my mindset for what was to happen, and to pave a way to the aftermath. While on the way to the hospital, I gave my answer, saying that I would not only be strong but I would also make sure that nothing would be left unfinished as long as I still had breath in me.

Right after New Years, in January 2019, I took time to respond to those questions once again, and then I mapped out an execution plan. I took note of all plans and dreams that I could remember, including our foreplaned charity work, and committed to wholeheartedly work on each item regardless of the heaviness of the pain I felt as I revisited them all.

The first part of the question had been answered during and after the mourning period and funerals. On that evening of Thursday, November 8, 2018, in the hospital room, I vowed to be strong, to behave as a true believer of life after death, and to be committed to live with purpose as long as I was still breathing. Of course, this was not a one-time attitude; it required my intentional commitment on a constant basis, to keep reminding my whole being to be strong. I remembered the psalmist who would command his soul to stop being downcast, but rather to trust in his God.

I learned, for the first time, to look at myself straight in the mirror and confess an affirmation on a daily basis. I am humble and grateful to God for his grace that enabled me to navigate through that intense moment of the excruciating weight of grief. The journey is long, and even though we are not yet where we are going, we are a long way from where we started.

Acquiring a Home

Our dream and plan to acquire a home in the Greater Toronto Area had been paused. After the unexpected had happened, I had a choice to make. Yes, we were well off financially and had already been approved, but now the income projections were no longer the same. Even though I would still be approved, the level of risk had become extremely high. I asked myself if I was really ready to add the big responsibility of owning a home without anything to fall back on, with two toddlers to raise. The incentive to own a home was also disappearing. I thought to myself, what is the benefit of having a home without a homemaker in it? It seemed to me that it would be impossible to make a house a home without a mother in it.

As unrealistic as it seemed at that time, the answer was not far from my lips. I proceeded with the plan. I had vowed to never alter any plan that was within my reach; it would be betraying the life we had been gifted with. On March 7, 2019, I locked in the purchase of my first home, with a closing date of May 30, 2019. I felt extremely happy, with a mixture of sadness, that this beautiful home would serve as our safe haven with the babies, but without Princess. At the same time, I felt that I had made the decision she always supported, and I knew she was happy with us where she was.

We moved in on June 1, 2019. Since the first day we stepped inside the door, our God has been faithful, and life has been livable in our home. We are able to host all sizes of gatherings with family and friends. It has become our Rehoboth, meaning "open spaces," for the time we are still around. This really has been a home; we celebrate and create memories with family and friends. Our home has been open from day one, and we enjoy hosting people.

Foundation – Charity Organization

When I was growing up, I always dreamed of running an organization that would impact and improve people's lives. Among the many reasons I fell in love with Estelle, the heart of service ranks the highest. Our dreams of helping others matched and it was a strong pillar for our marriage. We started spreading acts of love towards empowering youth and counseling different people, including couples, and helping marginalized people, especially in Rwanda and Congo. We agreed that once we were settled and our babies were a bit more independent, we would start a faith-based charity organization, where we would use our talents and resources to empower others.

During my conversation with the invisible voice in my car, it was crystal clear that the time had come that I put into action what we had always dreamed of. It was a wake-up call to never postpone anything that I can do today. I could not afford to see the dreams and plans I so dearly shared with Estelle be silenced with her.

*"The pain of losing Estelle was too much to waste.
So, I chose to work on every project with my last energy."*

So, as soon as we had returned from the homecoming ceremonies in Kigali, I started working on incorporating a foundation. I registered the Heart of Worship in Action foundation (HOW Foundation – www.howfoundation.org), and it was officially incorporated with the province of Ontario, on June 28, 2019.

You might wonder about the rationale behind the name I chose for this noble organization. Princess and I shared many passions; I would think that every couple does, but the main two passions we were both passionate about were worship and empowering people. When we started composing our songs, we gave our home band the name "Heart of Worship." We did not have plans to do worship music to make money; we just wanted to pour out our hearts in reverence to the giver of life. As I mentioned earlier, we also enjoyed serving others through different channels. Princess, especially, would come up with all kinds of initiatives to put a smile on someone's face, and she always made sure it was done anonymously.

When the time came to register a name for the foundation, it was obvious to me that this foundation was an extension of what we had started doing many years back, so I added the word "in action" to form the Heart of Worship in Action Foundation. What we had been doing anonymously and informally, was now to be put into visible actions.

After the incorporation with the province of Ontario, I also registered the HOW Foundation as a charity organization with the federal Canadian Revenue Authority Charity Directorate office (charity number: 77330 8879 RR0001). This milestone has positioned the organization to fully operate at national and international levels, contributing to the betterment of our society.

Through the HOW Foundation, we have been able to reach hundreds of people. We have empowered marginalized women and teen mothers in Rwanda to start income-generating activities, and helped over 500 children in Mulenge, a remote area of Congo, by providing basic needs. I know Mulenge well; I was born there. I get joy that can't be traded for anything when I see a small act of love that speaks volumes to people who have barely anything. One such act is the shelter we built for an elderly survivor of the 1994 Tutsi genocide in Rwanda. Seeing how happy the father was to have a small house to call his home, made me tear up with so much joy.

I have big plans to continue making small impacts, one at a time, through this foundation. I strongly believe in the power of access to skills and capital. When these key factors are available to someone, regardless of where they live or the life conditions they are in, by having direct access to adequate skill sets and capital, they can take actions that will change the course of their lives for good. That is the HowFoundation, and that is what we will continue to strive for. With the support of our partners, we will faithfully and accountably carry our mission to the next level. You can support my charity work by purchasing items from my website at www.WhenLightFadesAwayHopeRemains.com.

Album Recording

Singing, and worship in particular, is what defined my relationship with Estelle. I started singing gospel in the Sunday school, and at age 12 I had joined the church choir; since then I have always been part of a choir and/or a gospel band. From the time we were in Zaire, when we moved to Rwanda, and then the Netherlands and Belgium, and now in Canada, I have been fortunate enough to continue doing what I love to do.

I had not written a single song until I met my princess. I believe she played a big role in my song writing journey. The first song I wrote back in 2006/2007 or so, was based on Psalms 139. It was late in the night, around 3 a.m., when a strong melody woke me up and I picked up my guitar (I could play a few chords) and started writing. The next morning, I called my fiancée and told her what had happened a few hours earlier. She asked me to sing the song for her on the phone, which I did, and she was extremely happy. She was so excited, more than I was myself, and she encouraged me to continue writing more. Little did I know that I had just awakened a new gift I did not know I had.

We then started writing songs together, or in solo, and then corporately finetuned them together. As we continued to write, even before our wedding, we started talking about producing them. As we discussed this, we both felt the time wasn't right. We both agreed to wait for the right time, when both our hearts would feel ready. We never intended to make it a career or a main source of income; we just wanted to have our pieces out there to be a blessing to those who would listen to them, however many they would be.

We continued to postpone this, year after year. Friends encouraged us to produce our songs many times, but whenever we talked and prayed about it, our hearts were not in agreement that it was the time to do so.

Fast forward, when the unexpected happened, I was convinced that it was time to produce the songs. A few years back, I had a dream about singing in a big stadium, with a big band and a choir backing me. I saw thousands of people attending that event; however, I did not see Estelle on stage with me. I told her about my dream and she quietly responded by saying, "Maybe you will be singing while I am taking care of the babies." We did not really dwell on it; we thought it was just a strange dream.

When I released the first song, on November 27, 2019—a song called "Izina Ryawe (Your Name)," written by Estelle—after a few weeks, it had a couple of thousands views on YouTube (https://www.youtube.com/c/WillyMGakunzi). I immediately remembered the dream I had a few years back; it must have been in 2013 or 2014. I understood that my soul and spirit had been preparing for the songs that we had been putting on shelves, to be sung when Princess transitioned to the other side of eternity.

I was encouraged to continue, and I completed my first album of 8 songs in 2022. These songs have reached thousands of people across continents, and my hope is that at least one person has been inspired by them. I am working on my second album, which I hope to complete this year. The majority of these songs were written many years back, between 2009 and 2018. I have added a few new compositions that are part of the first album and the one I am working on.

Singing has been one of the strongest things to help me in my journey of coping with grief. I will continue to sing as long as I still have breath in me.

Serving at My Home Church

Three months before the unexpected happened, we had decided to become permanent members of the Church on the Queensway, in Toronto. We had been attending this church as visitors for over two years, and during this time, we were just members who attended all activities but did not volunteer in any capacity. We did not want to rush adhering to the membership of the church because we wanted to make sure we were making a thoughtful decision. I am a strong believer in the transformational message of the gospel of Jesus, so I needed to commit to a community with all my conviction.

After a time of prayer and studying the doctrine of the church, we were convinced to take the next step to make the Church on the Queensway our home church. We also had decided that once we became members, we would both start serving on the worship team. When the time came to register for the auditioning, around August 2018, Princess surprised me. She told me that it would be a good idea that I start, and she would join once I started. When I asked why she thought that it was best that I start, she responded saying that she believes in the family hierarchy; therefore, because I was the head of the family, I should start, and she would support and join me later. She also added that this was going to be "your church," which sounded like she was not part of it anymore. I did not understand what she meant until she left. She was telling me that this was going to be the home church I would attend, with the girls, without her. It was so hard to comprehend. I wondered if she somehow knew that she had only two months left.

When the time came to gather my energy and continue living with the bigger picture of life in my focus, although I had so much on my plate that demanded my 100% attention and commitment, I also decided to continue serving as a singer and guitar acoustic band member for the worship team. The times I serve, both with the main services and the children's department on Sundays, feel recharging, and it yields hope to my soul.

Missing Love Letter

The next morning, I woke up without her love letter, and it felt like a spear had pierced through my heart. I was confused and doubted if I would make it to the next day. My daily energy booster was nowhere to be found. I started revisiting the archives and continued to journal without any reply. How hard and heartbreaking did this experience feel? How can this shift from one day to another, from overflowing with happiness and contentment to grief and pain? Only love that was lived in perfect harmony could become my place of comfort.

The memories created rekindled the dimming light without my princess at my side. How long would this go on, I wondered. Some days it felt unreal to believe, but as time passed and I did not see or hear her affirming words, the unbelievable became facts. Would I give in and break altogether? What if she is watching and cheering me from the other side? I felt her voice saying, "It will be okay," the exact words she would say when we were going through life challenges together. I would hear her sweet and tender voice praying for me before I went out for work. Indeed, prayer is like a seed you plant but don't eat from its branches until months and years after. It is the faithful messenger you send to your future, and you find him waiting at the door to usher you in.

The memories we had built together, the love we lived in action, and the seal of prayer for each other, in one accord, are the tripartite that hold me and the babies firmly and help us be hopeful for a brighter future.

Love Letters

Journaling and sending lover letters to my princess was a very emotional draining exercise; however, it was very effective in expressing myself in a free and authentic way. There are heartaches that you can experience but fail to explain by speaking. When you are grieving, there are constant conversations ongoing in your heart, mind, and emotional tanks, and failing to express them can lead to undesirable results such as depression and the like.

Most of the time, the victim—the person grieving—is scared of not being understood, especially when cultural factors are involved. A man is to be strong and not show his weakness and emotions. A man should not cry; his tears should flow from within. These are some of the myths that I grew up hearing, and I was trained to behave accordingly. It is also uncommon practice, especially in my culture, to see a man raising his children alone after losing his spouse. All these factors were becoming inexpressible, and the weight continued to increase within.

I was caught in between. How do you live up to the cultural and societal expectation, and at the same time express your pain in a way that does not end up destroying you in your vulnerable state? It takes a strong emotional power and gazelle intentionality to keep the balance. I would hear some comments that would break my heart into pieces, not because the comments were bad in nature or they were being made with bad intentions, but because of the need, or craving, to be understood. Those well-intentioned comments would really hurt, leaving you with intense inner loneliness.

It comes naturally that when you talk to a single parent, especially after the death of one of the parents, people tend to worry about the children.

So, I would get calls, and the first question was always, "How are the girls?" Allow me to be vulnerable here: This question goes into the heart of one hurting as a sharp spear. I never answer that question using "they." I always quietly and gently respond with "we." So, my answer would be, "We are all well. Thank you for asking."

What this question really communicates to a hurting heart is that you should be strong, and babies are the vulnerable ones. You are an adult; you should be over it by now. In many cases, I would find time for myself and just pour out my heart, crying like a baby.

"Communicating with a grieving individual is more effective when spoken words are less or not used at all. Presence in all its forms, physically or by virtual check-ins, is the most effective communication channel."

In this state, the only person I trusted that would understand me, even in the absence of spoken communication, was my princess. But because I was not able to show her my facial and other physical communication expressions, I chose to start writing her letters. These letters are in the form of narrating my days, my feelings, and at times asking for her advice about different topics. I felt her presence and was well understood. I will not share all the letters I have written in the past five years; however, I have selected a few I deemed fit for our conversation in these pages of the book.

May 8, 2019 – Six Months of an Uncertain and Frightening Journey Without You

Dear Princess,

Today marks exactly six months, to the day, that we are without you in our lives. It was on November 8 ,2018, around 1 p.m., that I last heard your sweet voice. Little did I and the babies know that you were about to travel to the other side of eternity where we would not be able to hear you or touch you. You were so happy the day you left. You had just accomplished what you had worked for so diligently. You had just graduated and started your new career. How did it happen that you left when you were so young and flourishing? It was so unexpected that I haven't realized that you will not come back.

I cannot stop thinking, at least wishing, that you would one day come and ask me how I am doing with the babies. Then I could relate to you how we survive each day without you, and about the cries and unanswered questions that go through our minds every single second of every day. I dream and wish there was a telephone number I could call, and hopefully you would answer me, and I would tell you how Kayla and Shayna are doing. It's been six months; how did it happen? How did heaven decide to take you when everything was settled for us? How did heaven allow Kayla, Shayna, and me to go through this agonizing period? I wish I could reach out and talk to you; I wish you had gone for a short stay, and you'd come back to narrate how life is on the other side. I wish we could reunite either way, here or there. I think my heart and the babies' hearts would be unexplainably happy. I simply wish you had not left. I wish you had stayed to laugh, love, live, and enjoy with us. But who am I to question all this? Did I plan the day you came into this world? Did I even plan and/or coordinate the day we met? Did I play any role in Kayla and Shayna's birth other than being a passive agent?

Now that all that I wish for cannot happen, at least in a physical and palpable way, let me tell you how these six months have gone by. From the time I received the call, my heart and body froze. I did not know what to think or what to do. However, there was a kind of peace that I did not know where it came from, but it certainly must have come from God. I started to imagine what I would say if the unexpected were to happen. I started to put my thoughts together on what I would say, how I would talk to Kayla and Shayna, and how life was going to change. All this came into my mind as a movie, but I could simply not imagine that it was indeed happening.

I was there in the room when you had no strength left to talk to me. I was there when doctors tried to keep you breathing. I was there, confused and powerless. I was there looking at how peaceful you were while lying down and trying to keep your breath. I could clearly see that you heard every single word I tried to express. I reminded you how much I loved you; I begged you to stay, and I know you wanted to respond but your physical strength was fading, and your time was quickly drawing near that you could no longer hold. I prayed, but heaven seemed to have turned its back on me as its whole inhabitants eagerly waited to welcome the princess that you are. The whole heavenly army had turned its back on me, and it was fully focused on the entrance gate where you were entering from. Does this mean that heaven had forsaken me? I don't think so; however, it had decided against my will.

If you remember, my last words to you were that of forgiveness. I wanted, so badly, to apologize for all the stupid and silly things I had done. I wanted to hear you say that you forgave me. I know I have loved you without limit and have never doubted your unconditional love, but I also know for sure that I had so many shortcomings, and I wanted to make sure that you went happily.

Every day since Thursday November 8, 2018, has been very different without you. I have started to imitate your cuisine; sometimes I succeed, but other times I just make something to keep up with life. Kayla tells me every day about how grateful she is that I cook like you! That encourages me but also breaks my heart knowing that she will never see you again walking on this planet. You know how good her memory is; she remembers everything, and she keeps reminding me of the things we used to do together, here and in Belgium. She is just like you. Shayna has grown into a big, beautiful, and extremely intelligent daughter of yours. She is as smart as you. With her dominant character, she sometimes imposes her own rules, and that can be very hard to cope with, especially knowing that you cannot tell me how to get around that. They both ask me very tough questions, being as smart as they are, and it breaks my heart that you will never experience that on this planet called Earth.

Five days after you left, Shayna turned three, and Kayla helped to organize her birthday party. I always make sure that everything they get or any activity we do, I tell them that it's what you wanted me to do or get for them. We now try to do activities that contribute to our happiness, but nothing so far gives as much joy and satisfaction without you around. After all, how can I be complete without you? How do I even make it to the next morning?

There is quite a lot I would like to share with you, but now I must run to get Kayla and Shayna from school, and then I will have to make dinner and find time to pray and play with them before we go to bed. But before I conclude this letter, I wanted to share with you some of the questions they have been asking me, and some of your dreams that we have carried and were able to accomplish.

Kayla asks: How will I live without Mummy? She was the best mummy in the whole wide world.

Shayna asks: Why did Mummy go to heaven without us?

Both ask: What will happen/who will stay with us if you go to heaven too, Daddy?

These are some of the toughest questions I deal with almost every day since you left. What should I answer? My common answer is that you are always with us even though we cannot see you, and that God knows best what awaits us.

You remember that we wanted to buy a home? Guess what? We finally found one that you'd have liked. The very moment I stepped into that house, I told Helen (realtor) that I was going to buy it because it's what you'd love. It's a three-bedroom, detached home, and it's very nice, especially the kitchen area. We are moving in on May 31ˢᵗ but I know it's going to be tough to live in it without you.

God has been faithful. I am hurting still but He gives me strength to carry on, and the babies are very healthy and happy, as you'd wish them to be.

I love you; I have always loved you, and I will love you till we meet again. On that day, for sure, I will give you my eternal hug. Till that day, please keep praying for us and please visit us in dreams. That would be very cheerful.

I moved the babies into our room so that we could console and comfort each other.

Love you Princess!

September 5, 2019 – My First Birthday on the Uncertain and Frightening Journey Without You

Dear Princess,

I am still in a stage where I cannot define it, and I am not sure if it is still a denial phase or simply an uncertain environment that I am trying to navigate in. For close to 15 years, this is the first birthday I am celebrating without you. I was so used to the surprises you would give me; it had become so obvious that I would get a text message, a kiss, an affirming word, a nice meal, and most of all, the beautiful look you would always give me.

Here I am trying to celebrate regardless, but I am still unable to process that this journey without you will go on for as long as I am living on planet Earth. I still ask myself if you knew that you were traveling to the other side, because all you did in the last three years seemed to point to the fact that you knew. Would it be possible that you had known the plan for so long and chose to keep it for yourself? I remember you telling me that I should get used to sleeping by myself. Was that your goodbye? Well, knowing who you were and how loving you were to me and the babies, it seems impossible that you would keep any secrets from us. If you knew the exact date and time, you would have said goodbye in an explicit way.

That said, however, I truly believe that your spirit and the spirit of God in you knew very well, as all you did and said indicated that you were about to leave. I sometimes wish that I knew then all that I know today.

Anyway, let me tell you in short what and how we've been doing up to now. Since my last letter to you on the 6th-month anniversary of your departure, we have been missing you more and more. Despite your physical absence, Kayla, Shayna, and I have been keeping up quite well because of God's grace. I tend to believe that you advocate more for us now that you are next to Him. Please continue to watch over us as you always did. There have been major changes in our lives, and those changes keep confirming two main points in our lives: God's goodness despite the void you've left us with, and the dreams you had for us all.

On July 28th, Kayla turned 8 years old. Can you believe that our Imfura is almost a grown-up lady? She resembles you more and more. By now, she looks exactly the way you looked when we were still dating. I am 100% confident and sure that she will grow up resembling you more and more, and she will live the life you did not live on this side. She is so sweet, responsible, caring, prayerful, and cheerful, just like you were, and how you are now that you are in the fullness of God's glory. Before she celebrated her birthday, we had acquired a big property in Ajax, Ontario. It is a very nice home that I am sure you would have loved and made it a home to raise your beautiful family. The day I saw it, I screamed to myself, "This is what Princess would have loved." I went ahead and put in an offer, and by God's grace, it was accepted. That's where we celebrated Kayla's 8th birthday. We had around 50 people on that day.

To conclude Kayla's highlights, she just started her grade 3 on September 3rd. She is attending a French Catholic school and she is doing very well. Every day, we pray together to proclaim God's cover and protection as she starts a new day.

Your youngest baby, Shayna, has grown and turned into the most independent, eloquent, loving, and joyful carrier in our family. She is so verbal and straight to the point. I see more of myself in her. Shayna defends everyone, mostly Kayla and me, whenever anyone tries to come around us. I cannot explain to you how much joy she brings to us. Whenever we feel unhappy, insecure, or sad, Shayna (remember she is only 3 years old) finds a way to make us laugh and forget what's around us.

Going back to November 13th, 5 days after you left, Shayna turned 3 years old. Do you remember that we were planning to go and celebrate her birthday at her school before you went to work? Well, since Father God decided to take you before that, Kayla and I joined Shayna to celebrate her birthday with her class. It was only 5 days after your departure, and your body was still at the funeral home. Princess, this was one of the hardest days I had to go through. I had to make sure I provided not only the protection the girls so much needed during that period, but I also had to put on a garment of joy to celebrate Shayna's birthday. As strong as she is, she enjoyed the time with her classmates, and we (Kayla and I) did our best to make her day enjoyable.

Shayna is now going to start school—can you imagine? She will join her sister, Kayla, at the same French Catholic school. She is so much looking forward to it. However, I have noticed that she has been a bit stressed lately. She cries a lot before sleeping, and I sometimes feel incapable of comforting her, but after all, God has never failed us, and He never will.

Now, back to today's celebration. As you know, I am not a fan of celebrating birthdays; in fact, I started celebrating when you came into my life. Fifteen years after, I have become so accustomed to it, and I miss you so much today. Despite all this, I have decided to celebrate today with the babies. I have, once again, decided to instill the values we taught them: celebrating and enjoying life with their loved ones. We are planning to go to the KEG restaurant. I guarantee you, Princess, that I will do my best to play both your role and mine in raising our babies, as long as I am physically with them.

As I am writing this letter to you, my heart has mixed emotions. I am happy to have been given additional days to fulfill my purpose for existence, but I am also in so much pain because I am alone without you here. It is so hard to fully enjoy things without you here. I tried to revisit the memories, but it also brought back the pain within. I felt so empty and wished to go back in time. I wished we could roll back the time and relive the life we used to live. I wish you were here to hug and go out for dinner together. I wish you were here to travel to Switzerland. The list goes on.

I am not ignorant or believe in staying in the wishing state. I know that you won't come back; rather, I will come to you when my time comes. I know that God's never surprised or confused; it would never be a mistake that He called you. I know that where you are, you probably don't have time to remember and think about what we are going through. You fought the good battle, you finished your race, and for sure you have received the crown of the good servant in your Father's house. Knowing this, I have decided to move on; I am going to try to dig deep to find the joy I can find, in spite of it all. I have decided to make the sacrifices required to raise the babies with the values we both shared. I once again promise you that I will do my best to leave the babies in a good condition and state of mind when my time comes.

Do you remember that you left us with so many friends? We have gained even more friends who are closer than ever before. We have been receiving so much love and care from all around. Frankly, if it wasn't for them, and of course for God's grace, we don't know how we would have made it. Today I have received so much love and best wishes from all corners of the world. Apoline made me feel the same way I felt when we first met. I received a long, loving, and assuring message from her and the whole Ruvebana family. I am telling you this to let you know that we are very well surrounded, even though nothing and no one will ever take your place.

I could go on and on and on; but allow me to conclude here by saying that we miss you more and more. We will always treasure your memories, and the prayers you sowed in our lives will bear many fruits. I will carry the torch until I pass it on to Kayla and Shayna, which I hope will be when they are mature enough to stand on their own two feet.

Till we meet again, I will continually miss you. Rest in eternal peace!

April 21, 2020 – Tough Time Parenting on the Uncertain and Frightening Journey Without You

Dear Princess,

By today, I had thought that it would be a bit easier to move on and continue living for you and for ourselves. Whenever I tell myself that the babies and I are a few miles ahead in the healing journey, I find we are falling back, and it feels as if you just left.

The void is huge, and the pain is deep to bear. Kayla has kept a memory of literally everything. She remembers even the little details that I cannot easily remember. This makes it hard for her to heal. Most of the time, when she lies down in bed at night, the memory and your image appears, and she starts crying because she misses you terribly.

It's Tuesday, April 21, 2020, at 10:30 p.m., and she jumped off her bed and ran into my room. She told me: "Dad, I was conversing with Mom, and it's really unfair that we are among the few kids who don't have their mother."

And then she continued: "Why did Grandma Domitila go to heaven for four days and then came back? Why can't my mom come back? I need her here." At the same time, baby Shayna tries to remember and repeats what her sister is saying.

Here I am, speechless and wondering why you can't come back. Is there another plan God has for your babies down here?

Then Kayla said: "Dad, I want to pray." Here's how she prayed: "Dear God, thank you for this life we have. Shayna, Dad, and I need a mother. Help us. Amen." We hugged and then I took them back to their rooms.

Here I am, and I am still not convinced that you have passed. I have a feeling that you watch over us. You talk to God on our behalf. It feels like you are just on the other side of the line.

We miss you tons. We love you forever. We will feel the void for the remainder of our lives here on Earth. We pray and we hope that one day we will sit and tell you all we went through without you.

Still love you just as much as the first day we kissed.

Rest in peace!

November 7, 2022 – Another Milestone on the Uncertain and Frightening Journey Without You

Hi Princess,

How are you doing up there? How is heaven treating you? I am sure, even though heaven is good, it has become even better with you as our guardian angel in it.

It has been four years since you left us. I remember this same night in 2018. We were celebrating your graduation. I remember what we talked about before bedtime with the babies. I remember we ate some ugali for dinner that night. I remember the joke we made before we kissed good night.

Wait… do you remember thanking God for having achieved everything you had dreamed of? Did you know you were going home the next day? Did you know we would be staying behind and would have to continue to live without you with us? Did you know?

I strongly believe your soul knew that it was time for you to go home. I do recall all the things you said and the events that followed. All of that confirms the fact that you knew, deep in your soul, that you were going home.

Princess, you did your part, and you impacted my life for the rest of my days on this Earth. I can only dream of the day we will reunite again. I know it will be me joining you at home.

Back to our life here with our babies, today we became Canadians. Isn't it surprising that we took the Canadian citizenship oath the same day you took your graduation oath four years ago? I believe that everything happens for a reason, which we might not always comprehend.

How I wish you were here with us.

The babies are happy to become Canadians; now we don't have to go to Europe for passport renewals before we can travel.

After the ceremony, we took time to remember you. Princess, it was so hard tonight. Imfura (first born) still cannot handle your absence. They asked why you left and, every time, I fail to give an appropriate answer. How can I explain things that I don't understand myself?

How is it possible that life keeps its routine without you in it physically? I still don't understand, and I do not expect to understand.

That said, God has been so faithful. We are well sheltered, well fed, and well dressed. We even manage to bless others with our overflowing cup.

God, somehow, manages to use these ashes for his own glory and in ways we cannot possibly understand. God has given us friends, some that you know and many more that you have not met. Trust me, God is good, and he always finds a way to reach to us. I am sure you know him better now that you hang around him.

Tomorrow, November 8th, will be the day your loving heart failed to give you enough breath to keep you alive. It hurts a lot to go through the emotions. But because of the promise I made to you that night in the hospital, I will stay strong and will be where you are not for our babies. And I will continue to do what we both loved till I give my last breath.

Princess, I miss you so much. If only I could see you one more time; if only we could hold hands like we used to do, and if only I could tell you all that I feel now.

Knowing that none of the above is possible, please keep praying for us that God will continue to be there for us. Now that you can chat, remind Jesus of your babies—we need his warmth more than ever before.

Je ne saurais pas conclure, saches que je t'aime toujours, comme le premier jour!

Till we meet again, I will still celebrate you.

Yours, Me

These are some of the letters I have been journaling for the past five years without my light around. There are many that are personal and not fit for a published book. However hard the journey to our healing and dealing with grief has been, journaling in a very open and vulnerable way, without fear of being misunderstood or judged, has been a power mechanism for my healing. Life has expanded around the pain and the physical absence of Princess. We are moving forward—not forgetting the past but building on a strong foundation that is rooted in deep pain that present and future challenges will not be able to shake. We are hopeful, and our focus is on the brighter light that gives light to life.

Navigating Grief with the Babies

Grief and the process of grieving is not something we get prepared for; it cannot be learned in theory to apply when the circumstances present themselves. As an adult, you try to make sense of the loss and the pain thereof, but even then, it is hard to find your path through because of so many emotions involved.

When it comes to children, not only is it so devastating, but it is also blurry; it does not make sense at all. I have seen my babies being fine and playful one minute, and in the following minute, they are crushed down and are going through pain they cannot even comprehend how to express. At the same time, I was, and I am still, mesmerized by their level of resilience. I still cannot fathom how my babies are so resilient in the way they navigate the loss of their mother.

I have a very strong connection with my girls—how threatening to think otherwise—and I am so grateful for this bond I have with my babies! Because of this connection, we communicate a lot through questions and answers. They ask me questions such as why their mother is gone, how they live in heaven, whether she sees what we go through without her around, etc. They even ask me what would happen if I also went, who would stay with them, and if I was also going to die soon.

I do not have answers to most of these questions, and they break my heart whenever we have such times. I listen to them, hug them, and reaffirm my presence until they can take care of themselves and of me, because they will at some point have to take care of their old father!

However hard it was to help them make sense of life through the grieving period, it has always given me joy and a sense of humility for the privilege I have to shape the lives of these gorgeous girls I have been entrusted to raise. When I see how they get confident after talking through these tough questions, I remain speechless and so thankful to God for his unending mercies in their lives.

Mother's Day

"What is the point of celebrating Mother's Day when my mum is not here physically?" Kayla asked. "I don't want to celebrate. What's the point?"

"I want to go to a restaurant for Mother's Day, and I will make crafts for Mum," Shayna echoed. It becomes intense as the two argue about celebrating this important day in children's lives.

Kayla is growing up; her rational level is mature for her age, and she has so many memories about her mother. The Mother's Day celebration is something she has experienced; she has planned and tasted the joy of celebrating her mother. Shayna, on the other hand, does not have any memory of that, so her reasoning is not related to an experience she can relate to. For her, she just doesn't see why we shouldn't celebrate.

It became more challenging as the years passed and both were growing. The first year and the second year, we were still celebrating; they would give me gifts and celebrate their mother, and I would also craft surprises for them, which made them feel okay. As years pass by, Kayla is more acute in the way she handles things; she knows the meaning of things in life and she is exposed to the external world with her peers. And her being the first born, she has a say in the house, so she challenges some of the practices.

As I watched them discussing whether to celebrate or not, many thoughts ran through my mind with issues of life questions. Then I turned to them and said, "I think it is a good thing that we celebrate. I understand how hard it is for us to celebrate your mother when she is not with us. Nevertheless, I think it is worth doing. But if you guys do not want to do anything, I will still celebrate because you are future mothers." The discussion ended without any conclusion. Kayla was still firm that we should not celebrate, while Shayna was still insisting that we should celebrate. I have to accommodate both demands.

The next day was school, and of course these events are talked about with teachers and other pupils. When they returned, they both came back with messages to their mother—Kayla's was written in English, while Shayna's was written in French. I will copy and paste:

"Hi, it's me, your daughter. I'm just gonna tell you my feelings about you not being here physically with me. Mother's Day is coming and I am sad because everyone is saying that they are doing something special for their mums. I'm sad and I feel so out of it, if you know what I mean. Like it's not fair for me. I always ask myself why you left."

"Bonne fête maman. Tu es une très bonne maman, tu as un grand Coeur, tu es la meilleure maman, tu es la plus belle, je t'aime de tout mon Coeur, je t'aime toujours."

These are the moments where you feel like the weight of the whole world is on your shoulders. Although heartwarming to see and know that my girls can express their feelings freely, it still leaves me wondering what in the world happened to us.

It's time to pick up the baton again and continue to plant seeds that will one day grow into fruitful trees—the expanded lives of our babies in the land of the living.

"The journey is never ending.
There's always gonna be growth, improvement,
adversity; you just gotta take it all in and do what's right,
continue to grow, continue to live in the moment."
~Antonio Brown~

"Even if I don't finish, we need others to continue.
It's got to keep going without me."
~Terry Fox~

Chapter 8

Picking Up My Pieces

There is a consolation when you see and live a result-driven life. The contrary is also true. When the gap between the things that are true and we truly believe in, and our life experience widens, it is almost impossible to attain consolation, especially after experiencing a life altering event, like the death of your loved one and the mother to your children.

Although nothing can and will ever replace a life in its entirety, when you live with tangible results, there is a consolation found in that life that has been disrupted.

I strongly believed that I was going to live a long life with Estelle and prosper together for a long time, to see our daughters attain the heights we had not been able to attain. I strongly believed and I was convinced that heaven would spare my children to live the life I lived of being raised by a single parent.

When I got married, I had earnestly prayed, and I felt heard that Estelle and I would live our golden years together. I had worked extremely hard for our marriage to grow strong amidst the different challenges I aforementioned, so I settled and I felt assured and firmly believed wholeheartedly that God would not fail me in that area and let us down by taking one of us so early. (My definition of God failing us in this context is for the lack of a better word; humanly speaking, I felt that I had the right to age with Estelle at my side. After all, all dimensions of life seemed to align with my conviction.)

I was successful in my career and was performing excellently. My princess had finally graduated and was working. Our gorgeous daughters were healthy and growing well, and our families were in harmony. God had blessed us with true friendship relationships across the globe. I mean, if you go to Africa, I can enumerate genuine friends, and in Europe it's the same. Now, in North America, our friend circle was growing exponentially, and even in Asia, where we had not yet lived, we had friends that we made through our life journey.

I could not have asked for a better life. All our plans seemed achievable, in time and cost. As I mentioned above, we were shopping for our first property in Canada. For those who know the real estate market in Canada, and especially in Toronto, at the time we were shopping, prices were very high. Nevertheless, we were qualified to acquire one.

My prayers had not been answered as I had hoped. I was now left alone—although not alone because God has never forsaken me—to carry on with life. The need to attain the consolation that stems from God through a life with fulfillment became more eminent. This life we so much aspire for does not always unfold in the way we expect it to. It requires that we contend for it. It requires that we follow predefined pathways in life.

So, I resolved to pick up my pieces even with the physical absence of Princess. The light had left from my sight, but it was not dimmed on the inside. I resolved to live and provide a life to our daughters that would have proven results. I refused to be defined and confined in the parameters of widowhood and orphanhood. I refused to lower my standards. I refused to live in despair, so I hoped.

However, hope alone is not enough, and by itself, results cannot be achieved. In addition to hope that provided joy to life, I resolved to follow the pathways to life by applying result yielding principles. I trained my mind and my body to keep focusing on the bigger picture of life, by staying consistent and striving to improve by just a few percentages each day. I knew that one day the compounding effects will kick in when the momentum reaches its climax. I also kept reminding myself of the available supporting systems and resources that can and would help me stay the course and pick up the undamaged pieces. I would not have been able to lift even a small piece without the determining factors I will discuss below.

"Pain does not reduce as time passes, but life grows and expands around pain over time, making it more and more bearable."

Solo Parenting

It is said that parenting is the highest form of leadership, and every stage of it is a new experience worth studying for the success of this parenting skill. Principles and values evolve as life circumstances change. When our daughters were babies, I was only worried about having them fed and clean. As they grew, the priorities changed; now I was more focused on their safety as they started moving and gripping things. I was concerned they might get hurt if a chair fell on them or if they touched a hot surface. Every stage of their lives revealed a new face of the parenting journey I was not aware of or prepared for. These dynamics are what make parenting so worthwhile, even though challenging.

Life had changed and they were growing. The growing patterns are still unfolding. However, the family dynamics have changed irreversibly. The attention provided and tasks performed by two parents were to come from just one, wearing both dad and mom hats. Sure, there are dishes to wash, a house to keep in order, hair to do and clean, homework, etc. The ultimate responsibility of growing leaders who will play their role in society had not been reallocated because of the circumstances we had found ourselves in, and as a father who is now also playing the mother role, this mission became even more pressing. I should pull up all the required resources to provide a solid foundation for Kayla and Shayna to grow into women that will live up to their full potential.

Although parenting responsibilities, combined with all other household chores, had increased on my to-do list, taking a little and intentional time to snuggle and enjoy the moment with my beautiful baby girls had been the number one priority that truly matters. The prompt hugs, hide and seek play sessions, evening walks in the summer, and home workouts were the moments that kept my batteries charged and kept me moving unaltered.

There are no secrets between me and my babies—I really pray and hope that this trend will stay the test of time—they know who I talk to, they know my phone password, and they still tell me their little secrets and struggles that they go through during their school days.

I am not ashamed to cry with them when necessary, and it has allowed them to freely express their emotions whenever they are stirred up. In addition, we agree to speak positivity into our lives. Each morning before they step outside to go to school, I remind them of how beautiful, smart, and blessed they are, and then I say a blessing over their lives. It's a rule in our home that we don't step outside before we say a blessing to each other. I figured it is imperative for me as a father to daily set the basis of their day's outlook. It does not mean things won't happen; however, whatever happens will find that the seed I planted is already taking root.

The harmony and good relationship we have between the three of us does not come challenge free. Some of my disciplinary decisions are questionable and can at times leave me with a sense of guilt. I question myself whether I could have done differently if life had not changed the way it did. Hard questions are encouraged to be asked, and in many instances, I do not have answers to them, but we have all learned to talk and then pray together.

Solo Parenting Amidst COVID-19 Pandemic

As the whole world stood still, not knowing what next steps to take, the human energy seemed to have lost it batteries. Human beings, for the first time in my lifetime, were afraid of each other. Everything became still, and what could possibly move was moving at a very slow pace. As the whole world became isolated, my babies and I felt it too. We were confined in our home 24/7 with no visitors for months.

Although I was working from home even before the pandemic, this work arrangement did not seem to help as the babies were also homeschooling. The already complex household management started becoming really hard to navigate. Managing the emotional toll of the pandemic, attending and helping the girls with their homeschooling, and continuing to working at an optimal level felt heavier and heavier as the days passed by.

Even though the world was still in isolation, the fear of infection and the possible consequences thereof started weighing my heart down. I wondered what would happen if I happened to get sick—who would take care of my babies and me? I wondered, if anything happened, what could possibly go wrong? The whole situation was paralyzing to me, especially when thinking about the possible scenarios that could play out.

We were spared during the peak season; the girls and I did not get infected. Towards the end of the crisis, in December 2020, as everything opened up, including travel, we used the opportunity to travel back home to Kigali, which was an opportunity to breathe and recharge. This was the very first time the girls had traveled back to Kigali since the homecoming ceremonies for their mother in 2018. It was a mixture of emotions, but overall, it was a very good experience for them.

Come May 2022, schools had opened up and everything was back to normal. The girls picked up the virus from school and shared it with Dad at home. We were all double vaccinated, but we still had a few days in bed. Kayla and I were the most affected, but after three to four days, we had all recovered.

This experience, from the beginning of 2020 to 2022 when we got sick, I was reminded of the goodness of God in our lives. Many families, including my extended family, had experiences that were harder and more heartbreaking due to this pandemic. It was a time to reflect on what mattered most, which is having each other around to create memories. It was yet another time to value and appreciate the life we had been gifted with. What an experience. How did we not break down? How did we manage to homeschool, work, and keep life balanced? We might not have clear answers to these and many other questions, but it's clearly because the light was still on. The source of true light that enlightens our lives is still open and accessible to us.

Award Winning: Orchestrated Life Path

As I continued to make my humble but committed contribution in my work, I did not realize how impactful it had been to both internal and external stakeholders. In the year 2021, amidst the pandemic of COVID-19, my team was tasked to develop a new solution for the new global banking regulation reforms that had been issued. Banking institutions, systemic global institutions, and domestic ones had received new regulations they were required to comply to. As a global solution provider company, we are expected to provide expert solutions for our clients, to help them meet their regulatory obligations. For the first time, my team, whose mission is to deliver the packaged solution to the client, was now tasked to develop and deliver the new solution, and under tight timelines.

With my two girls were homeschooling during the total lockdown, I had to find a way to effectively and efficiently divide myself to satisfy all the demands. Managing two school-aged children, with all side effects that the pandemic imposed on us all, was a full-time job in itself. I had to be there for them one hundred percent as they navigated the online homeschooling approach, and at the same time, I had to continue to do my work with a global team in different time zones.

I prayed and prayed again to God for help. I prayed for energy, for peace of mind, and for unwavering happiness, and then I continued doing what I was doing, focusing on the next right thing on my to-do list. I continued following my daily routine—going to bed on time, waking up early to work with colleagues in different time zones, finding time to exercise, finding ways and time for fun with the girls, and making sure life in the lockdown could still be enjoyable. I intentionally kept myself in check to not commit to my work at the expense of my quality time with my babies, so I would always log off work on time, and I limited working past work hours or on the weekend.

Every year that followed after Princess transitioned—2019, 2020, 2021, and 2022—I have been moving up the ladder to my current position as a country manager for our professional services business, to serve the banking industry. I strongly believe in hard work ethics, and I heavily rely on the principle of favor from fellow humans, and honor is due to those I serve, my team, and my clients. I have made my mind to excel through constant and continued self-development. The grace of God, the true light, and the light that my princess and I shared, have been the enabling factors that have seen me succeed through the ashes of grief.

Without realizing it, the year 2021/2022 were the years that I exceptionally performed, and I was awarded the outstanding leadership CEO global award. This is an award that is given at the global division level. Employees nominate individuals who have demonstrated exceptional leadership traits and have impacted the business as well as the well-being of both the employees' and customers' experiences. It is a very competitive process; to win, you have to have a very high number of votes. The nominations are anonymous and there is no campaign for it. Colleagues have to take time from their busy schedule and nominate you, not knowing who else has been nominated. Only the CEO office sees who has been nominated and the reason behind the nomination.

After receiving the announcement of this surprising news, the whole movie of my life journey played back in my mind, including the scene from that hospital room in Belgium 8 years prior, when I was about to turn down the offer. I felt the weight of loneliness; I felt the palpable absence of Estelle. She was the person who cheered me even in my weaknesses; she was the very first person in my entire life who saw my worth and affirmed it in words and actions. Here I was, in my home office alone after receiving this great news; it suddenly felt bitter, and many questions arose in my mind.

I questioned myself if I should rejoice at all. After my emotions had cooled down, I reflected on the grace and goodness of God. I was reminded of the light that was dimmed but never turned off. I picked up my pieces; I shared the news with my friends and family who genuinely celebrated with me.

I was, once again, reminded that love is more powerful than death. How we love, the seeds we plant in those we love, and the memories we create are our true legacy that outlives us and provides the real life meaning to those we leave behind when we are gone.

I was also reminded that when God helps a man, there is nothing he cannot do, despite the circumstances. God orchestrates events whenever he wants to honor someone; not because they are able, but because God's mercies are on them. When I felt weak and incapacitated, the highest God showed up, and through men, I was trusted to do what I did (with my team), which turned out to be a pathway winning an award. This particular event was a reminder that I was not alone even though it felt lonely most the time.

I dedicated the award to the love and memories I had shared with Princess through the work of my foundation. Because of this award, I was able to provide the basic necessities, such as shoes and clothing, to more than 500 children in Kakenge village (birth village), in DR Congo.

Friendships– New and Lifelong Friends

A friend loves at all times, and a brother is born for adversity, the wise say. I have always understood the value of friendship—the ones you know you can truly count on; however, I had not fully grasped the true value of genuine friendship up until I lost the other half of me. I had not understood the importance of friends that bear your burdens at the time of vulnerability in your life. The friends that I had grown so accustomed to and, at times, had taken for granted, showed up and became true burden bearers. Yes, I am a social person by nature, although very reserved, and I have always been, most of the time, on the giving side of the relationships. I have been a good friend that cared, comforted, and in many cases, sacrificed for others. This is not to say that my friendship relationships have been one-sided, but rather to illustrate the fact that I had not experienced the imperativeness of having true friends that stick around through thick and thin.

When my shoulders had become weary, when my energy was at its lowest level, and when I most needed help but did not know how to ask for it, my burden bearers showed up—those I knew and many new friends that had been added to my life. I speechlessly observed how my friends gave up their obligations and made sacrifices that only friendship could explain.

The experience of losing my life partner revealed the other side of friendship that I had not fully grasped before. In my friendship loyalty mindset, I always felt compelled to be the giver. I discovered and understood one of the weaknesses in me that I was not aware of. I was someone who did not easily accept being celebrated or cared for. I always thought that it was a bit too much for people to go the extra mile for me, whilst I found it commonsense to do extra for my friends and those I care for.

When I needed my friends the most, they all showed up—those that I had and many new ones that heaven had sent my way. It mesmerized me to see how far people can go just to make sure you are well; just for the sake of friendship.

I have a close circle of friends that shared life memories with me as a young and single person, and later on as a couple and family. I always knew that they were the people I could count on, telling each other's secrets and failures, and celebrating each other's successes. When Princess transitioned to the other side of eternity, I truly understood the level our friendship had reached. These are individuals and couples that I can unashamedly say that they are my friends. These friends knew my princess and I while we were courting, and we journeyed the married life together. When I think of them, I truly see them as a part of my life. Their presence in my life has tremendously helped in picking my up the pieces after the loss of my light.

Lifelong Friends

Dr. Etienne Ruvebana and Apolline Ruvebana – Etienne and I attended the same university in Rwanda, but he was senior to me. We later connected in the Netherlands in 2006, when he was doing his master's studies at the University of Groningen, and later in 2009, when he was going for his PhD at the same university. I was also studying at the same university, from 2005 through 2008. At that time, he was courting Apolline, and I was courting Princess. Etienne and I became friends, and our to-be spouses became friends as well. We shared our student life challenges, our dating complications, and later on our family life.

After getting his PhD, Etienne moved back to Rwanda, and his family joined him after some time. Despite the distance across continents, and the moves that both our families had made, we stayed in touch with the Ruvebana family . When Princess passed on, the Ruvebana family proved to me once again what it means to be friends. My kids know Etienne and Apoline as their uncle and aunty, and they are truly so. Our friendship with the Ruvebana family is beyond just friendship; we have become a family.

Their home in Rwanda is our home, and vice versa. Their presence in our lives through the years, and especially during the loss and grieving period, has stood the test of time. You can have genuine friendship regardless of the time and distance.

During the two weeks we spent in Kigali for the homecoming ceremonies, brother Etienne and sister Apoline and their children were the family that our kids knew and could trust to be with. Every time we travel to Rwanda, it is a given fact that we stay with Dr. Ruvebana and his family. I sometimes take their friendship as a given fact, simply because I know the place they have in my heart and the one we have in theirs. This is true friendship, indeed.

John and Darlene Mutebutsi – John and I have known each other for over two decades now. Our elder brothers attended the same schools and were good friends too. We both found ourselves in the Netherlands and started our pursuit of a better future together. We studied the same program at the University of Groningen, and we were in the same class. We also co-rented our student apartment. During my first encounter with my princess, John was there, and he continued to be there (sometimes being closer to my fiancé than I was, as they had become sister and brother). Princess and I played a big role in John and Darlene's relationship as well, and once we were all married, it was almost impossible to separate our families. Till today, if anything happens to John and Darlene's family, I am among the first to be notified, and the default expectation is that I will be there, and vice versa.

During the tragic passing of Estelle, John coordinated all activities in Canada and Rwanda, while being in Belgium. Both John and Darlene also traveled with us for the homecoming ceremonies in Kigali. Nine months later, John came to see his nieces and me, and he spent a whole week with us. This is what I call friendship. At times, I feel like it is their duty to do what they have been doing, but then I remember that there is no such obligation, other than true friendship.

Francky and Gody Ngabo – I had heard the name Gody during the first few occasions I spoke to Princess, when I was dating her. She told me that she had one best friend in life that she wanted me to know and accept as her best friend, if I really wanted to build a life with her. Gody and Estelle had been friends since elementary school; they went to the same high school and became inseparable. A few years later, Gody got the opportunity to join us in the Netherlands and attended our wedding. Princess wanted Gody to be at her wedding, and God made her dream come true. When Gody met Francky, she told him that their relationship wouldn't be formal until she had gotten approval from Estelle. We were so happy when she presented us the man of her life. Although the same age, Gody became like our daughter, and she was also an aunty to our girls at the same time. She became like our daughter because we were the ones who gave her in marriage in 2015. I walked her down the aisle and Estelle was her maid of honor. Francky came to consolidate our relationship and we have been a family since. One year later, we had moved to Toronto, and Gody and their daughter came to visit, which I interpreted as the time the two lifelong friends, Gody and Estelle, had to say their goodbyes. Gody is the godmother to both Kayla and Shayna, and although we live in different countries, we are in constant contact. She is the aunty Kayla and Shayna know as a sister to their mother; up until recently, they thought that she was a blood sister to their mother. This is the power of true friendship.

New Friends

The apostle John wrote a letter in the New Testament, to the people he loved, and he wished them to prosper in all ways as their souls prospered (3 John, Chapter 1 verse 2). As I journeyed through loss and grief, life never seized to prosper my relationships. I understood that one of the ways that prosperity is measured is by the level of health and good relationships one maintains. Relationships can buy what money cannot buy, and they can provide consolation in times of need.

When we moved to Canada, we did not have close friends in the new country we had embarked in; all that we knew was left behind in Europe. I remember, two weeks after we had arrived in Toronto, Kayla asked us why we had spent two weekends without anyone visiting us, or us visiting anyone. Everything was strange and new to all of us. We had a few friends and acquaintances across Canada but did not know anyone in the city. As I dug into my emails, I reconnected with a couple of friends from South Korea, Byeong and Su-Jund, who we had met in the Netherlands. We reconnected and they introduced us to the church that became our home church.

As social as I am, I started initiating conversation with people I met; I invited them home and, in some instances, I invited myself to their home. This was the start of new friendships that became as strong as family.

Andrew and Barbara Bukuru – We met the Bukuru family at church, as we walked outside after the service. I saw a group of people who seemed to be from the Central-East African region. I walked up to them and introduced myself and my family. I asked where they were from, and they happened to be from Uganda. We exchanged telephone numbers, and that was the start of our friendship. Andrew and Barbara became our first genuine friends we made in Toronto. We started organizing family get togethers at our homes; from there, we met other friends that I will describe below. When the unexpected happened, I remember texting them and, in the next few hours, they were with us at home. Andrew did the eulogy at the service we held here in Toronto before traveling to Rwanda for the homecoming ceremonies. The Bukuru family have been with us since the day we met in 2016 to present, and we are still involved in each other's lives as true friends. Their friendship was a great support as I started picking up my pieces after my light had gone. They are the people we celebrate our small wins with.

Dr. Denis and Peace Semwogerere – We met Denis and Peace at Andrew and Barbara's place in 2017, and we immediately became close friends. A few months later, we hosted both families at our place, and the rest was history. This is a family that loves truly and enjoys hosting a bunch of people at their home. Whenever we meet, be it at their place or at our place, the earliest time we depart is around 3 a.m.. A few weeks before Estelle passed on, we had visited them, and we all took a tour in their van, shopping for our house. They had planned, without us knowing it, to take us around the Mississauga and Oakville areas for open house visits. When I texted them that the unexpected had happened, they immediately came and stuck with us through thick and thin. Denis is one of the friends who really asks the questions and makes sure he knows you are well. He makes the conversation simple and deep at the same time. This couple has been there for every milestone we have reached, and we continue to celebrate our small wins together. Both Peace and Denis inspire me and teach me the meaning of meekness—very small and accomplished people that reflect a sense of meekness and genuine love that leaves you in wonder—checking if I have balanced my approach. I am forever humbled and grateful to have you in my life.

Pastor Maombi Lisa – Maombi is my maternal niece, who I had an opportunity to see once in 1998 when she fled the war in Kinshasa and came to Kigali. Her mother, my cousin, Apostle Domitila, is a global icon. She is the living person that died for four days and came back to life. I knew my cousin but did not have any relationship with my niece, Maombi. I saw her one time when we had moved to Canada, and the next time I saw her was when they came to see us when Princess passed. From that day, Maombi became my confidante; we cried together, and she embraced her cousins—my daughters—and they identified with her as their trusted sister, and to some extent, she is a mother figure to them. Maombi became more than a niece; she indeed became my best friend. We share each other's struggles and celebrate each other's wins. She has gracefully and patiently navigated the loss with us, yet she never had a chance to meet or know Estelle in person. A friend is made for adversity. Thank you yaya.

Pamela Mutijima – Pamela is a new friend, sister, and confidante I gained towards the end of the year 2020. Pamela has known me since the passing of Princess, through her aunty, who is married to my uncle-in-law, the paternal uncle to Princess. She attended all the ceremonies and had most probably greeted me but we did not know each other. We met in the fall of 2020 and became friends indeed. Her family, children, and husband have all embraced us as part of their family. Pamela is that stubborn friend with the powerful gift of listening. Her friendship is one of the best encounters God has placed in our path, and she has brought so much joy to our grieving hearts. She knows when to affirm and bring out the best in you. I remember when she surprised me with an award in appreciation for having played my part as a father and friend to many. She made me realize that even when we doubt ourselves, the small things we do matter and can make a difference. She is my friend to stay.

It is impossible to name each and every one who's impacted our journey through friendship relationships. My three lifelong friends and the new lifetime friends I have gained before and after the passing of my light, are the people I know, beyond any reasonable doubt, that will pick up my calls at any time of the day, from anywhere in the world. They are the friends that will bail me out in any circumstances. Their friendships and their unwavering love and patience have provided strong and reliable shoulders I have leaned on as I continued to pick up my pieces, as I navigated through grief and my quest for a future full of hope.

They are a representation of many friends across the globe that I have had the opportunity to know and journey life together throughout my lifetime. You have all played an integral role in shaping and, even more so, sustaining my life balance after the loss of my other half. I will not be able to name each of you; nevertheless, I treasure your friendship. You have helped me become a better person through our encounters.

You have helped me understand and value the power of true friendship even more.

Family and Social Duties

I am, by my upbringing, a family and community person. I was raised up to fight and strive for my family values, which when preserved, reflect my community and cultural values. We succeed together and also face challenges together. I grew up in a very close and cohesive community where children were raised by the whole village. As I mentioned in the first chapter, my father was a noble community leader. When he passed on, although I do not have many memories of the event, the whole community came together to help and continued playing a big role in our lives after him.

Having left my village life at a very young age and transitioned through multiple cultures, I still find myself not understanding fully all the cultural rituals, especially when it comes to family matters. As much as I am very cultural and hold dear to my cultural values, I oftentimes find myself in conflict with the way things are done or expected to be done from my culture's standpoint. When I became a widower, the cultural tension became more palpable, as my view of life did to a certain degree differ from that of my family and community. This is not to say that there is anything wrong whatsoever with my culture's rituals—far from it. It is, rather, a realization of how much my life has been carved by different other cultures and life experiences I had been exposed to. There are habits and norms I have unlearned along the way as I adopted new ones. Many of these cultural conflicts became more pronounced when I was left to raise the babies as a single parent.

In addition, although I am the second youngest of eight brothers, I took on family responsibilities at a very young age. This added much pressure on my shoulders as I knew the domino effect my breaking down would have on my entire family, and especially my mother in her old age. In the beginning, I struggled a lot to find the right balance in dealing with my grief, while I helped my family to navigate their own and, at the same time, keep playing my role and assuming my family responsibilities. It was not easy at all. I knew how much my siblings and mother were suffering because of my situation; this put so much pressure on me, to the point that I had to keep my emotions within lest I hurt them. Through open and transparent communication, they slowly understood me and continued to journey the trail together and in harmony.

My family had also been increasingly concerned with my well-being and ability to raise my daughters by myself. In their concerns, which were very valid ones, they resorted to the cultural approach, which did not always match with my views and life context. I had evolved towards the independent way of living, which in my situation of now being a single parent with the girls, could very much weigh on my well-being. I was caught between having to live up to the cultural and family expectations and approaching my new life as I saw fit.

I reached a point where I was becoming less patient. At times, I felt not well understood whenever they brought my case up in our family calls. Some of the cultural practices were coming into conflict with my personal beliefs and principles. I realized that I had to take actions and constantly keep my state of mind in check. During the course of my life, through education, work, and life, I had been exposed to different life standards, which had all shaped and changed me. All the dynamics in the play necessitated a recalibration, especially on my side. It was up to me to sit in the driver's seat to help my family cope with the new life journey we had all embarked on. With this mind shift and by the love that binds us together, and the favor bestowed in my life, we started experiencing the joy once again.

I committed, with the help of my family and those close to me, to meet my social obligations: making my contribution in family matters, including paying school fees for those in need, and continuing to live collectively as opposed to being isolated. It goes a long distance when you don't stop living because of adversities encountered. Life has much more meaning when lived in togetherness, even amidst the shadow of grief.

I would not have been able to navigate the intense emotions of the grieving process without my family and close friends by my side. I would not have been able to carry the unbearable and heavy pain of losing my other self without the support of my social and church community. I would not have been able to provide and nurture my babies without the favor and mercies of the giver of life, through the faith and hope he gives every morning. I would not have been able to excel and perform in my work duties without the hope that illuminates the path of our lives. I would not have survived the loss of my light if I had not put my faith in the light that shines brighter than the stars.

Decision Making

Decision making is the hardest process that one who is grieving goes through. From deciding on how to daily go about every activity, to making a decision to move on in life, everything becomes blurry. You become less confident and unsure about every step you take in life. In my case, it had been 14 years, day by day, that I had not made any life decision by myself. From the day we started dating and throughout our married life, we made all major decisions together, be it in regard to finances, family, relationships, investments, or our spiritual commitments.

After Princess transitioned to the other side of eternity, I became so insecure about my decision-making process. It became so hard in my thought process to identify whether what I was doing was the right direction or not. Even when I knew that I was moving as we had planned, there was always a voice in the back of my head that doubted my moves. I wasn't sure anymore of when I should spend or how much I should spend. When it came to raising the girls, I questioned myself so much on whether I was instilling the right values or not, especially because they are girls. I still think that I see things through a man's lenses, and this does create a huge weight of doubt in my thoughts.

I started revisiting what we used to do, how we proceeded in implementing certain decisions, and the steps we took. The challenge with this approach is that life changes and circumstances evolve over time. The approach that yielded results in 2018 might not necessarily lead to the expected results in 2023, not because they are wrong as approaches, but rather because life's circumstances have evolved over time. Kids are also growing; the toddlers are now preteens and teens, so how do I adapt without my light to validate and advise or question the approach altogether.

There was no one-solution-fits-all, so I stayed the course. I tried my best to focus on the current state, taking one step at a time, and making sure that no major disruption was introduced along the way. With the help of God, friends, and family, we slowly moved forward. As life continued to expand around the pain, the grief became more bearable, and life started to become sweeter, with enlightened hope for the future.

One of the greatest lessons I've learned from all of this has been to take life one step at time, make room for failure, and be cognitive of the learning process. Seeing results even when you have doubted your process gives consolation and motivation to move forward. I will still be learning as long as life continues.

Love the Enabler!

I wondered, and still wonder, why I suffered this much in my life. Why do people in general suffer? Although I am not an expert in the subject, speaking from experience, I reached a point where I flipped the question and redirected it to myself. I kept asking why, but I did not get a logical answer, so I changed it and asked myself, why not?

When we love a person, at first glance, it seems like they are faultless and infallible. We don't see their shortcomings or the possibility for them to not deliver. At the same time, we are fully aware that the person we love so much can eventually fall sick; they can fall down and break a bone, or anything can happen to them. Yet, because of the love we have for the person, we commit, and we truly love them.

The same applies to parents. We wish and pray for the fruits of our love, which are our children, knowing very well that the children we raise, might be bullied at school. They might fall sick and spend a night at the hospital. Even when we don't actively think about it, somehow, subconsciously, we know that they might die.

All these very well-known, obvious, and possible challenges do not prevent us from making these decisions solely based on the love we have for them. We marry and allow our wives to go through so much labor pain because of the love we have for the children we will raise. Wives willingly go through the excruciating pain of labor in the name of love.

As these life examples dawned on me, I answered the "why not me" question: "Because of love, I can go through pain and eventually see light on the other side." This realization has been a powerful enabler in my daily life. I am hurt and heartbroken but not crushed to the point of not continuing living the life I have and enjoying the many blessings therein. Love does not end when we die; rather, its memories become the strong foundation we continue building the future on. Because I have loved and I was deeply loved, I am able to write this memoir, and I look forward to continuing to effectively live my life with purpose for the rest of my days.

I have picked up the pieces of my life, and my foundation is deeply rooted. The hurt heals!

"When someone shows you who they are, believe them the first time."

~Maya Angelou~

Chapter 9

Who Was Estelle?

W ho was Estelle, as a person and friend to many? What was her character, personality, values, beliefs, and principles by which she lived her life? I have requested a few people who have known her in a deeper way to share their perspectives on how they knew her. I believe that by doing so gives a more accurate picture of her memories. In fact, I asked them to write their testimonials without even revealing what the title of the book is, nor the message therein, to make sure I did not influence their content. My goal in not revealing the concept of the book before they provide their views was, on the one hand, to give them an opportunity to share their story, because I know they do have a story to tell; on the other hand, I wanted to minimize and, where possible, eliminate any bias that might arise from my side. Yes, I can openly—which I hope I have achieved through the whole memoir—talk about Estelle as my wife, and about the life experiences we shared. However, when talking about her as a person, I figured it would add value when those who were fortunate to court her contribute too. For this reason, I will keep my part short.

Character and Personality

While personality represents who the person is, as a whole, character represents the person's ethics, morals, attitudes, and beliefs. Estelle was characterized by the highest form of integrity and honesty. She was the same person in private as in public. She was unable to pretend to be someone she wasn't. Apart from being my wife, she was the first person to exemplify the meaning of integrity to me. She was very honest in her dealings and her speaking too.

In addition to her sense of integrity and honesty, Estelle was loyal and generous, to a level that inspired security in anyone who came close to her. She was very careful to not over commit to many things or make promises; but when she did, nothing would change her mind or make her reverse her commitment. When she told me that she would marry me, she also made it clear that it wasn't for a trial period: "I am in it for life, and you can count on my loyalty, regardless of what comes ahead." She was loyal to her friendships and never complained about anyone. She was loyal and had integrity.

Estelle was a very generous person. Estelle was able to proactively identify the needs in people's lives before they themselves could, and she would come up with creative ways to meet their needs without making it known. In most cases, she wanted to remain anonymous or organize surprises with a team and never show up as the initiator. I know many families that she helped regain their lost romance and helped revive their marriages. She would identify who was not playing their role as they should in the marriage, give them ideas on how to treat their spouse well, and in many cases provide the financial means to facilitate the process, and then she would retreat so that the spouse in action would get the credit.

She always wanted our family to be generous, and she has indeed taught me to be generous. She made sure that we would have many people coming over to share meals with us, almost every weekend. She was a giver by definition. Since I met Estelle, to the last day of her life, she would make sure that anything new she discovered—new lotion, make-up, new recipe, etc.—she would tell her friends about it. If you were to ask the ladies who knew her, they would say that whenever she saw a deal anywhere, she would make sure that everyone close to her knew about it. I remember when we moved to Canada; she used to video conference with her friends and share with them the new cuisine recipes or toiletries she had discovered here. She made me spend money on those and send them express to the people we knew in in Europe. I can truly say that she has planted a seed of generosity in me.

Values, Beliefs, and Principles

Estelle was a woman of strong beliefs and principles, built on the highest form of values, such as respect, hospitality, love, joy, and genuine happiness. She strongly believed in family norms. Estelle was a strong and unashamed believer of the gospel of Jesus; she lived her faith in action and gracefully impacted many lives. She also had strong principles by which she lived her life and has helped me develop mine. Estelle did not measure her worth by material possessions; she knew who she was and confidently lived by that, whether we had enough or when we were lacking. I remember when she would wear the same dress over and over when we did not have means, and she never complained about it, nor did she compromise in any circumstance, before or after our marriage. She also did not have to give up or alter her firm convictions for the sake of pleasing me as her husband, before or after marriage. What she believed in remained constant for the 14 years she was in my life.

Estelle also loved and respected people in their different levels of life—poor, rich, young, and old, she paid everyone their due respect. For all the fourteen years I courted her, dating and as a couple, I have never heard any rumors about Estelle's misdealing with people. She did not joke about life, nor did she take anything that involved her name lightly. And that applied to her family; she made sure, as my wife, that I lived up to my word. I owe her my transformation, and for life. She made sure that every word she spoke, every action she took, and every move she made, were seasoned with grace to bless and positively impact those who interacted with her, family members, friends, and strangers.

Estelle was beautiful, inside and out; she was devastatingly beautiful. They say that beauty is a relative term, to which I do not disagree; however, when the outward appearance of beauty is combined with a pure heart, the relativity aspect of beauty loses its pertinence. Estelle was pure in heart. Estelle was beautiful physically, and with this, not because she was my wife, I can straight and tall testify that she was beautiful.

Estelle was prayerful. She prayed for everything you can think of. She prayed even before breastfeeding the babies; she would thank God for the grace she has received to give birth and be able to produce mother milk to feed the baby, and then she would breastfeed. She even prayed before trying a new pair of shoes she bought. In her last two years of her life with us, from 2016 to November 2018, she had a routine of taking one week each month to go off grid and spend time in prayer. When I asked her what her prayer requests were, she responded by saying that she just wanted to spend more time with the love of her life, Jesus the son of God. She also took every Friday night as vigil night to pray alone in the living room. I would join her for a few hours only and then would take off to bed. I felt secure and unstoppable whenever I went out to work to provide for our family, because I was strongly supported and deeply loved. When she left, you can imagine how the foundation felt shaky.

Finally, Estelle was wise. I can boldly and unashamedly say that through her wisdom, I became a better person, a better friend, a good father to our daughters, and a good husband to her for the nine years I was privileged to live with her. Whenever I ignored her wise advice, I ended up facing consequences and wasting time along the way; but whenever I yielded to her wisdom, the results were unquestionable and in a short period of time. I did not know to what extent my light had shone brightly in many lives. She counseled so many people, who came out to pay their respects when she passed.

If I were to describe Estelle in one word, it would be WISDOM!

I promised to keep my part of this chapter very short, so I will let you read what those, who have known Estelle as a close friend and family relative, have to say.

Etienne and Apolline – Who Estelle Was to Us!

Etienne Ruvebana – The first thing I would need to note is that the exercise of writing a single script on Estelle is not an easy one for me. This is not because there is not much to write about her. It is rather mainly because it is impossible to write anything about Estelle without being emotionally worn out and drained. There is a lot to write about her, and it is difficult to select what to write and what not to. More than that, writing about her when she is no more is a painful and extremely sad exercise, which makes it difficult to put words together.

Secondly, it is important to know how I got to know Estelle.

I first met Estelle in 2006, during my master's studies at the University of Groningen in the Netherlands. I met her through Willy Gakunzi Makuza, who was also studying at the same university. I had known Willy since a couple of years back when he was still residing in Africa. During that time in Groningen (2006), Willy was living with John Kinyoni, whom I met then as well. They were living in the same house. Estelle was visiting them regularly, together with other friends, and I had occasions to get to know Estelle really well.

How did I connect with Estelle individually?

Getting to know Estelle well did not take long. We connected quickly and we became like very close siblings. She soon called me her brother and I called her my sister, and we lived by that. Willy was a very good friend as well, and so was John. Since Willy appeared to be dating her by then, I would call him my brother-in-law, and I continued to do so even after he married her in 2009. I had the privilege of being in their wedding in 2009. By then, I was doing my PhD at the University of Groningen. Since I was living in the Netherlands for my studies, our physical, virtual, and digital interface was regular as they continued to reside in the Netherlands as well. Even when they moved to Antwerp in Belgium later on, nothing changed. When my family joined me in the Netherlands, both my wife Apolline Kampire and my daughter Vanessa Uwimanzi were warmly welcomed and easily integrated within our trio-families' strong relationship, i.e., "Willy-Estelle," "John-Darlene," and us. Estelle was very instrumental in making this possible.

But who was Estelle if I were to describe her in a few words and lines?

This is a tricky question to which I will try to answer with the risk of not being able to find the exact words to accurately describe her without diminishing who she was.

To start with, Estelle was a symbol of love. Ever since I got to know her, I found her to be a loving person. Of course, there are other people who are loving, whom I have met. But what was special and unique about Estelle was her way of expressing and showing it. By seeing her, be it at her home or as a visitor, she would show you pure love. And she lived by that love. For instance, in all conversations I had with her, she would never miss the opportunity to say that she loved me, be it in a face-to-face conversation, on a phone call, Skype, or WhatsApp.

Being a loving person entailed being a very caring person, with a warm and welcoming heart. Before I drafted this script, I went back to some of the charts I had with her. In most of them, she was the one to start the conversation. This means that she would ensure that she got to know about our whereabouts. Her heart was always thirsty for knowing how we were doing on a very regular basis.

Also, Estelle was a civilized person but in a modest and humble manner that would make her be able to accommodate any person. This is always a very good combination that many people are not lucky enough to have.

More to the above, Estelle was a genuine and honest person. Whenever you would have a conversation with her, she would display the true image of herself. You would not doubt a single word she would utter since she was really a true person, not a pretender, whatever the circumstances. She would speak from the heart, and you would see the truth in her words and deeds. As such, I found in her an extraordinarily loyal and reliable person, which is difficult to find in many others. It is rare nowadays to have a person with such a pure soul. That is why she has left a hole in me that can never be filled.

And she was pleasant in attitude in such a way that you would always be fulfilled when she was around. She had a sense of humor, and she would make people around her feel her presence when she was around, and they would miss her absence when she was not there.

And in fact, with the above attitude, she was also generous in her warm home. In our culture, it is not common to praise someone for providing food or drink or the like. But at the same time, it is a very good value for someone to have generous hands and thus be able to take good care of the people around them at home (be they visitors or not). That is why, whenever there was someone who was otherwise, she/he would be known by everyone as such, and people would barely come to his/her home. At Estelle's home, she would always warmly show the desire to offer something, and that something would be served with love and without the fear of being impoverished.

It may perhaps appear to go too far to say that she was a person who loved her nuclear family to the maximum. To some, this may sound natural and thus be like stating the obvious. Be that as it may, it is worth noting that she would do it in such a way that everyone would see that their couple/family had strong pillars. It was unshakable. She loved and respected her husband in a very nostalgic way. And she would always advocate in his favor even in his absence. I remember that one day I had a long conversation with her. And there is one thing that our friend John and I used to complain about Willy (her husband), but of course in a teasing way.

Estelle told me, "Etienne, my brother, I want to tell you one thing. I know my husband Willy very well. If there is one thing I am certain about, it is that he loves you. And that is for sure without any joke." Of course, I didn't have the slightest doubt about Willy's love for me/us, but I was so touched by the way she testified in his favor in such a genuine and loving manner. The way she did it would have erased any doubt, had I had any. This shows how she had understood that the pillars of a strong relationship in a couple include love. But it also indicates how she understood that what makes a relationship strong includes having strong values. Estelle had unshakable, good values. This was a source of inspiration on how to build a strong relationship in a couple. The example I noted above is part of what shows how she would stick to displaying the good image of her husband. Willy is a very good person. But like others, he has not reached the level of perfection. Yet, I had never, ever heard Estelle criticizing him to others. This means that she had also understood that secrets are a strong value and a strong pillar in building a strong relationship.

Let me just say that her character and attitude made her be a person I found deserving of my friendship and brotherhood at all times. Indeed, even after I left the Netherlands and went back to my home country, Rwanda (after I completed my PhD in 2014), the distance did not affect the pace of our interaction. That was the same, even after she later moved to Canada with her family.

Then came her sudden death on November 8, 2018, which occurred in Toronto, Canada, where she was residing with her husband Willy and their two daughters Kayla and Shayna. With our very strong bonds, one would wonder how Estelle's sudden death impacted me.

On the morning of November 9, 2018, I received a call from my friend John Kinyoni. It was very early in the morning. When I answered it, I heard

John screaming. This made me get extremely scared and completely confused. Of course, I could sense that something terrible had happened. Yet, I could never imagine that it could be something that would be related to Estelle. I kept asking, "John, John, John, John, tell me, what happened?" And then I heard him mentioning Estelle, but just her name. Then I also started to scream, even before he told me more. As I continued to ask him, he later managed to pass on the sad news that Estelle had passed away. I cannot find words to describe how devastated I became. It was extremely painful. I cried unstoppably and I became extremely weak, physically and emotionally. Though I could not describe that pain in a much more accurate way, here is a paragraph that I managed to write as I was crying in my bed that whole day. I addressed these few words to her, and I posted the paragraph on my Facebook wall on the day after:

"Dear Estelle, our lovely friend, our lovely sister, our lovely everything. Unbelievably, you are gone in such tragic and sudden circumstances. I wish I had had a chance to see a sign or indication that you were leaving us such soon. Of course, there is not much I could have done. But I could have at least reiterated to you how much I and my family members love you. This is the only way we could have said goodbye to you. We have not been able to show you the amount of love we have had for you in the same manner you have done it. Your love and your way of showing it has been unique. You were such an angel. Your heart was so clean, warm, encompassing, and capable of truly giving joy to everyone, and it is beyond my belief that this very heart can't give any breath anymore. You were one of the most human and agreeable people I have ever known in my life. Your life has been well lived, but it has been made extremely short. I have completely failed to accept that I won't see your smiling face again, hear your unique laugh, and feel your loving heart again. We are deprived of having you enjoy life with your husband Willy and your small kids, with us, in many ways. If I had a chance to ask God a few questions, I would legitimately ask him a lot about you and the plan he has for your husband, your 2 little kids, and each of us. We can't say goodbye to you, Estelle. We can only say that we love you and we always will, and we thank you immensely for the true person you have been for us. Your very last profile status on your WhatsApp, with a picture of me and my whole family (which I can't stop looking at), will always be one of the sundry souvenirs from you."

This was the little I could say with the deep agony of loss I was going through. She remained in my thoughts, and the sadness was even worse whenever there was an occasion to talk about her. For instance, on her birthday (16th of March), I would dedicate a few words to her. Here are a series of examples:

On March 16, 2020, I wrote this on my Facebook wall:

"On a day like this (16th of March), years ago, an angel baby was born. She grew up and lived impactfully and contributed to creating other lives. This date has always been celebrated happily as her birth anniversary. At a given point in her quite young age (Nov. 2018), however, God (we are told) decided to take her soul back to him, without any notice and without a reason at such a young age. We have tried to face the reality of living life without her around us, but the hole in us has remained unfilled. On the date (today) she was brought to Earth, we do not have someone to say happy birthday to. Nevertheless, our hearts are thankful to her parents, who brought such a person to Earth (and to us). Likewise, we thank her again and again for the happy life she lived (with a pure heart full of love, integrity, honesty, compassion...). We will always reiterate our love to that lovely sister Estelle Gatera Gakunzi (now resting in peace). We love the family she left as well, i.e., Willy and little Kayla and Shayna."

And on the 16th of March 2021, I noted this on my Facebook:

"The 16th of March!!!! We were happy you came to life; you gave life and happiness, lovely sister. You are forever loved and missed."

And on the occasion of her birthday in 2022, I noted something in French. I am not a poet, but this time I thought to write something that is close to a poem in another language, French. It is another language in which I love to dedicate something to someone that I loved:

"Il fut un moment dans le temps où celui qu'on considère comme étant l'Être supreme ait eu l'idée de créer l'un parmi les êtres semblables à lui. A travers ses mécanismes ordinaires cela a eu lieu à une date précise et mémorable. Cela fut un moment extraordinaire car les éclats de lumière que sa présence/vie a donné en illuminant sur tous ceux qui lui ont été proche ont été brillants au point de s'imposer à la vue de toute personne et cela compte tenu de leur qualité inimaginable. Il est communément dit que 'tout ce qui brille n'est pas Or'. Mais dans le cas d'espèce ceci est paradoxalement tant vrai que faux. C'est (littéralement) vrai car les éclats de cet être ont evidement brillé alors que cet être n'était pas de l'Or (bien qu'ils aient brillé de loin plus que l'or, et donc pas comme de l'or car sa valeur est incomparablement Supérieure à tout ce qui a de la valeur matérielle). Mais c'est aussi faux car l' ironie qui est dans ce langage commun ne s'applique pas à cet être; étant donné que ce dernier a été incontestablement plus que ce qu'on pouvait s'attendre à un être dont certains croyaient être ordinaire. Que tout ce que nous ne pouvons pas comprendre à travers les moyens ordinaires nous le comprenions par voie divine. Que du bonheur à l'être à qui la référence est faite et que de la foi et de l'espérance à tous ceux qui lui sont chers à jamais. Que la date à la quelle la référence est faite ait toujours son sens et sa valeur. Etienne"

With the above, one would wonder how I coped with the loss, i.e., how I managed to process the grief.

This question is difficult and heavy in itself. And the answer to it is heavier. The loss of Estelle has taken my joy in many ways, and the grief remains fresh. What may sound strange is that the more the years pass, the more I need Estelle in my life. I am unable to explain why.

When Willy was in the process of establishing the HowFoundation (Heart of Worship in Action Foundation) as an initiative in Estelle's memory, he asked me if I would be willing to be part of it as a member of its board. I gave a positive response. Not only did I wish to be a part of anything that concerns Estelle, but I also thought it was going to be a source of therapy for me. But I later realized that I gave the wrong answer to the wrong question. In fact, the question would not have been whether I was willing; the question was whether I was able. And the answer to that question was that I was not. Indeed, the more I engaged in that foundation (after it was established), the more I felt deep anguish, until it got to the level where I had to openly mention to Willy that it was extremely difficult for me.

Even when writing this piece, I thought it was going to be therapeutic. But it has not been.

I think, and this is my final word on this piece, Estelle was part of my life. And as long as I live, she will always be part of my life. I thought I would recover from the grief, but I have realized that nothing can take it away. All I need is to cope with how to live with that grief for as long as I live. The only thing I should ask God for, is to help me see her in another life at one point.

Apolline Kampire – I first saw Estelle in 2011, when I first visited my (then yet to be) husband, Etienne, in the Netherlands. But she had spoken with me several times on the phone since 2010, before I met with her. I was then studying in the Philippines, but Etienne had introduced me to her (and Willy, John, and Darlene). That was the same time I met with Willy, John, and Darlene, the best friends of my (then to be) husband. But they used to talk with me on the phone since we were not living in the same country. I was studying in the Philippines, and they were living in the Netherlands.

I will try to describe how I found Estelle, i.e., the person she was. I found in Estelle a God-fearing woman, a good wife, a good mother, a good daughter, a good sister, a best friend, a counselor, and a comforter. She was such a precious person.

As mentioned above, it was in 2011 that I visited the Netherlands, and I met Estelle, Willy, John, and Darlene. I connected easily with Estelle because of her warmth and generosity.

I once read somewhere that there are 5 categories of people for whom we should always be thankful. The first is the category of people who will worry about you. The second is the category of people who can correct you when you are wrong. The third is the category of people who care about you. The fourth is the category of people who love to see you smiling. And the fifth is the category of people who tell you the truth even when that truth may hurt you. My dear big sister Estelle has done all this to me, especially in telling me the truth regardless of whether I would like it or not. I remember when, after we had started to talk on the phone when I was in the Philippines, but before we physically met, there was a time I posted something on Facebook. She called me and told me, "Apolline, despite your age, you need to remember that you have changed your status.

You are now engaged. And if I were you, I would not do that post." It immediately clicked in my head, and I said, "Yes, let me delete the post." In my heart, I said it is really rare to see how someone could be so sweet and tell me such an important truth before we even met. She was so happy that I listened to her, and she told me, "Apolline, ndagukunze kurushaho," which means, "Apolline, I love you even more." From that day on, I knew that I had a friend on whom I could rely. I wish I would have told her how this touched me.

Another thing worth noting about Estelle is that she was so creative. Her delicious recipes and her amazing surprises to her family and friends were exceptional. Her decorations and cleanliness were unique, and her tone of voice and laughter were so pure.

I could observe how she would put everyone's needs first so that she would see that everyone was happy. She was a peace maker. I learned from her actions. In fact, I would say that she lived, and I watched.

Regarding our relationship as couples, it was just amazing. Estelle welcomed me in this journey of married life and motherhood. She would always check on us. In particular, I remember that when I was pregnant, she would always send me an SMS, asking me how I was doing, especially in the last trimester. For instance, the day I gave birth to my son Sheja (which was 3 days before my due date), Estelle sent me an SMS in the morning, around 8 a.m. She asked me, "How are you? Any change, any pain? Any unusual thing?" I told her that my lower abdomen was hurting. I said that I was perhaps hungry. But she told me that I should watch out and keep track of it, since it could be contractions. And yes, she was right. It was indeed the contractions. They became so intense later on that I could not continue to communicate with her in the next hours. I gave birth at 3 p.m. on that same day. Estelle followed up otherwise. She was so caring.

The long distance was nothing to her when it came to caring about her loved ones and everyone in general.

One week before she passed on, I was not feeling well. I had anxiety and I had back pain. But since I had a newborn baby (who was then 3 weeks old), I thought it was normal to feel that way. But again, I asked myself why it was not getting better but rather getting worse. I did not know that I was waiting to hear such bad news.

On the morning of November 9, 2018, around 5 a.m., I saw John's missed call. I thought that maybe he had accidentally called me. I didn't bother calling him right back; I was going to call him back around 7 a.m. But he had also called my husband, and my husband called him back before I did. It was around 6 a.m. when we heard the devastating news that Estelle had passed on.

When I heard this, I got so many questions in my head. Why Estelle? What would happen to her husband and her beautiful young daughters? I did not have any answers. I said that only God knew. I said that I was sure that the God that she had served her whole life would have good plans for her loved ones.

I have always thought in my mind that I wish I was near Estelle's family so that I could spoil members of the family she left. But then I say that despite the long distance (Rwanda to Canada), I will try my best to be there whenever they need me, to provide my support in one way or another and to be the best aunty to her daughters, to guide them in every step of their lives. I loved Estelle; I love her and will forever love her.

John and Darlene – Who Estelle Was to Us!

John – In September 2016, I dropped Willy, Estelle, and the kids (Kayla and Shayna) at the Brussels airport and saw them off as they moved to Canada, where Willy had just been transferred by his company to manage a big project for their customer in Toronto. Estelle was the last one to wave back to me before they embarked. On my way back, I found myself sobbing uncontrollably in the car. I have had to say countless goodbyes in my life, but for some reason, this one felt the heaviest of all. Sometimes I wonder what I would have said to Estelle that day had I known that it was going to be the last time I would see her on this side of eternity!

Before meeting Estelle in 2004, I had known Willy for a long time. Not only had we become close friends, but I considered Willy to be like a younger brother to me. We went on to do the same study program at the same university (University of Groningen), sharing the same apartment. At some point, our apartment became so popular that some friends called it the African Students' Embassy in Groningen. But our apartment was not only open to African students; we were open to everyone, especially to HOST (Hospitality for Overseas Students) Bible study meetings every week. Strong relations and friendships emerged from those Bible study meetings.

In the meantime, we met Estelle. They didn't wait long before they started dating. But due to their Christian values, both put strict rules on their relationship. What we didn't realize then was how high Estelle had put the bar to protect this relationship and her own reputation. Willy and I once tried to convince her to join us in Groningen to pursue her studies, but she turned the idea down. She didn't want to move to Groningen lest the proximity with her fiancé would create an unwanted outcome! Estelle had become like a sister to me as well. So, I was very angry at her when she turned down our advice. But being who she was, her values and reputation mattered more than anything else.

My personal relationship with Estelle wasn't dependant on her dating Willy. It was stronger than that. Estelle had truly become a sister to me. According to some people, there was in fact some physical resemblance between us—perhaps because both of us were tall and skinny at that time (oh, how that made me proud!), and we would joke about that, especially teasing Willy, and sometimes we even introduced ourselves to new friends as brother and sister, and they believed us! Getting to know Estelle was like a prayer answered for me. I have always wondered what it would be like to have a sister around. I never experienced having a (same blood) sister. With Estelle, I learned what it was like to have a sister around. We could laugh, cry, sing, fight, love, and "hate" each other, just like a real brother and sister.

Things got even more exciting when Darlene and I got into a relationship. This was just a few months before Willy and Estelle's wedding. I was (logically) in charge of their wedding preparations, and my mission was to make sure the ceremony would be like no other. It was my brother and sister's wedding! And I can be proud to say it was the best wedding ceremony I have ever seen! One of the highlights of the ceremony was the song "What a Friend I've Found," which the four of us (Willy, Estelle, Darlene, and I) sang together. Two years later, it was Willy and Estelle's turn to take responsibility for organising our wedding ceremony.

A couple of years later, we all moved to Belgium in search of better career opportunities.

The first few years in Belgium were hard for both our families as it took longer than expected for both Willy and me to have our professional careers take off. But having each other made it easy for both our families to go through the hard times. Estelle's faith and continuous positive attitude made sure we didn't give up. One of Estelle's greatest gifts was listening and observing, especially when a friend was going through hard times. She knew exactly when to talk and when not to, and when to just listen. She would look at you and immediately notice when you were having a bad day, and whether you liked it or not, she would make you talk. Darlene and I will never forget the day we decided it was enough; I was going to leave Belgium and go somewhere else to look for job opportunities (although we didn't really know where!). Estelle and Willy radically opposed the decision. The next morning, Willy made a call to their human resources director. Later that week, I was invited to a job interview that would become the entry door into my professional career in IT.

Due to different events in life, she had put a break in her study journey. Fortunately, when they arrived in Canada, the first thing she did was to resume her studies. I was proud she chose to follow a program in the software development field, meaning she was joining my field. And so, we had a lot to talk about throughout her whole training program. Sometimes Willy would even "complain" about our long calls. She successfully completed her study program. The day before her graduation, we had a long call and she asked me what I was going to be angry about since I could no longer be angry at her, now that she had completed her study. I'm not sure if I made clear enough how proud I was of her. What I didn't know was that this call was going to be our last call before her graduation into eternity! Two days later, we received a call from Willy that would change our lives from that moment on. Estelle was fighting for her life in intensive care! We prayed, cried, and begged God not to take her, but everybody (God included!) likes to have the best with them. A few minutes later, Estelle was gone!

There will never be words to express how hard dealing with Estelle's passing was and still is. I've seen hundreds of close friends and family relatives go, but this one was unique in all aspects.

Darlene – I met Estelle for the first time at the church. At that time, she was in the choir and had a wonderfully beautiful voice. When I later also joined the choir, I got to know her more and more. She was very sweet and kind to me, along with Willy. I was the youngest member of the choir at that time, and both Willy and Estelle were always there for me. I became closer with Estelle when my husband John and I started dating. Estelle, Willy, and John were very close friends. Estelle always made sure I felt at home in the close friendship they had, and that I wasn't the fifth wheel on the wagon. By the time John and I got married, we had become so close that I couldn't think of any another person who would be suitable to be my maid of honor.

Even when she was far away, in Canada, the distance did not diminish the way Estelle showed me love. I still remember the day Estelle called me to ask if I was doing well. I was indeed not doing well. To this day, I still don't know how Estelle could possibly have known. Having a sister who could even sense my emotions from afar, is one of the things I miss about Estelle.

Dear sister, we were just given the privilege to write a few lines about who you are to us; however, as unachievable as that task is, you were and still are the light we carry within. If there could be some consolation to our grieving hearts, it would be to let you know that we love you still and we treasure the memories shared on this side of eternity! You remain a sister every sibling would dream of; a daughter every parent would be blessed to have, and a friend whose smile that was contagious to everyone who encountered your presence.

Till we meet again for the eternal party together, we love you!

Claudine Gatera – Who Estelle Was to Me!

In 1982, my parents welcomed their fifth born child. As the second in line, I was old enough to understand what was happening. My second sister was born, and she was special from the day she saw the sun. She was special to the point that we nicknamed her Dada (sister), as if she was the only girl in the family. She came after myself and my other siter, Pauline, but for some reason I did not understand, we decided to call her Dada. I came to realize later in life how special Estelle was as I observed how she lived her life.

Estelle was so peaceful, even as a baby. Her smile was contagious, and everyone at home, even visitors, wanted to hold this beautiful and peaceful baby we had been blessed with. She grew up wanting to help other people; even when we would be playing as siblings, she always put us first. She was happier whenever she managed to make other people happy.

As a teenager, Dada developed a strong passion for prayer. She prayed for us all and she made sure she would let us know that she was praying for us. She had become a strong pillar and the person to go to for advice. Dada's wisdom was beyond her age and even her education level. She was my resting place and my confidant, even though she was very young.

Dada's beauty, inside and out, was beyond comparison. What made her so beautiful was not just her physical appearance; it was her loving heart, which reflected a sense of peace, acceptance, and trust that we could not understand. Dada would make sure that we were all well. She made us laugh through her jokes and contagious smile. This was what made her so beautiful.

I remember that the same day she transitioned, we were chatting in our family group. It was late here in Kigali, but it was still afternoon in Toronto where she was. She sent us a message and, as she always did, she concluded the message with this: "Imana Ibarinde," which means, "God protect you." Yes, we were used to reading this every day from her, but this one came as a special prayer for us who were to stay. She did not want to leave without committing her family into the protective hands of God. This, indeed, is what we hold on to as we continue the journey after her. I love you, Dada!

In this chapter, where a few friends contributed, I aimed at giving you a glance of who Estelle was as a person. There are people we encounter in life whose mission is to impact us in ways we cannot stay the same. Estelle was that person to me. Her impact was beyond my boundaries as her spouse. As I meditate on why she impacted me the way she did, as she did to many, I never stop wondering what could have been the secret behind her personality. I strongly believe that she had discovered a secret sauce that provided light in her life, to the point that she was able to share the effects of it with so many that encountered her. Turn to the next chapter, where I discuss the source of my LIGHT.

"Truth will ultimately prevail
where there is pains to bring it to light."
~George Washington~

"When foundations are being destroyed,
what can the righteous do? The Lord is in his holy
temple; the Lord is on his heavenly throne. He observes
everyone on earth; his eyes examine them."
– Psalm 11, verse 3 and 4

Chapter 10

Psalm 11 — When Foundations Are Destroyed

I now realize my light and my father spent the last two years of their lives in the same manner—they both spent their last two years of their lives in the same state of mind. Both spent two years in an intensive time of prayers, depriving themselves of sleep and other life enjoyments, and yet they lacked nothing tangible. I always wondered if these two special individuals in my life had something in common. What had my father and my wife discovered that compelled them to devote to prayer fervently? Could it be that they knew that their time was near, and they wanted to invest in the future of those that would survive them? I strongly believe, although they might not have known exactly how and when their time would come, their souls did know with certainty. And because they had received that light that shines brighter than stars, they yielded to his will and prepared the way for us to walk into it through their prayers.

"Prayer is the only messenger you can send into your future;
when you get there, he will be waiting for you at the door
of your future and usher you into it."

I asked myself so many questions when my friend, wife, partner, love, etc. passed on. I questioned my faith in a God who keeps his promises and hears prayers. I questioned why I should hold onto my faith in the God who seemingly failed me, by allowing death to take the dearest person to me and my children. Was he powerless to heal; couldn't he perform miracles? How could a loving God who answers prayers let this happen to me and my two daughters?

Where Was God?

In my questioning period, I still devoted myself to prayer and Bible reading because I wanted to make my case to God. My father passed when I was just two years old and, as result, I missed many things in life that every child deserves to have. I never had anyone to call Papa, which is a wound that healed when I became one. So, I made my case and wanted God to explain to me how he could be so careless to make me and my daughters go through the same experience.

In my quest for answers, I was struck by this short Psalm, specifically two verses, 3 and 4. My foundations had been destroyed. I realized and comprehended that in this life, foundations can be destroyed. The writer of this Psalm did not question if foundations can be destroyed, but rather asked a question on the attitude one should have when the foundations are destroyed. He is giving us a factual statement that there will be times when things will go in opposite directions, and he also indirectly acknowledges that we will question the actions to take.

As I continued reading, the writer did not leave us with this factual statement only; he also gave directions on what the righteous person should do.

He gave us an illuminating truth that God is still on his throne in heaven, where he has always been even when the foundations were there.

In other words, these verses were telling me that my question about where God was when I lost my foundation, was not really the right question to ask. He, God, was and is where he has always been.

It also dawned on me that God was not idle, nor was he caught off guard when I was hurting. He was on his throne. And he observed and examined my ways. He examined my attitude. He observed my behavior. He observed my trust in him. The end of these few lines shows me that God did not only observe; he also sustained before and after the fact.

Surrender

As this shocking truth struck me, I felt disarmed and powerless; all that was left for me to do was to surrender. I allowed him to mold me, mend my heart, and carry me through my heartaches, which he did in an amazing way. This Psalm ends with another powerful statement that the Lord is righteous; whether I am hurting or celebrating, his righteousness is not affected by circumstances. The writer continues by saying that the Lord also loves justice, and those who are upright will see his face. I concluded that, if he loves justice, there is no way he was going to let me down. The question that remained, although I was still processing my grief, was how to make sure that I see the Lord's face in my daily life. I wanted to make sure that all my endeavors were backed by the grace and mercies of God. How would I secure this after my foundation was completely destroyed? The answer was to surrender and yield to his will. This, to me, is what being upright means in my life: not leaning on my own understanding and strength—which I did and do not have—but fully trusting his good plans.

"When I could not trace his hands in action, I chose to put my trust in his loving heart. He has not forsaken nor left me unassisted."

God's Faithfulness in Action

If you would have asked me five years ago to testify to God's faithfulness, I would have, most probably, given a different answer, or I may have even doubted his fidelity and his intentions. The vision and sight for the future was so blurry that I could not see or feel the expression of God's love and faithfulness. As I was hurting, I felt the right to not accept the fact that God was still faithful and loving even through the loss and the pain thereof. My trusting heart became cold and heavy like stone. I avoided, at times, any thought that would rationalize or try to comprehend that the loving God was still on my side.

Needless to say, God has been faithful. I have seen and lived the faithfulness of God in action. As I write this section, I am reminded of how life has been enjoyable with my babies. I have seen them grow in stature and wisdom. I have seen how resilient they are. I have seen how future driven they are. I have seen how lively their lives have been. Had it not been for God's mercies and faithfulness, we would have lost track and may have given in to despair.

There have been big milestones achieved in the lives of the two young ladies left to be raised by an unexperienced father. Helped by God, we three have enjoyed the blessings that stem from the same God who dwells in his holy place, observing and examining our ways. Kayla has just graduated her elementary school and Shayna is halfway. Who could have convinced me, five years ago, that one day they would both be independent and able to make decisions with me. Who could have convinced me that one day we would celebrate Kayla's graduation with so much joy and expectations for the future?

I can truly say that God has been faithful. I can unashamedly testify that we have been helped by God.

THE LIGHT

There must be a pure, true, and powerful light that illuminates natural lights that we see with our sight. That true light can only be seen through nonphysical eyes, and that's why, when we encounter people that brighten our lives, we do not see that brightness through our physical eyes. We interpret the impact of that pure light from a different standpoint, from within. We understand what the true meaning of our lives is through the reflection of this light in their lives.

Light is defined as a natural agent that stimulates sight and makes things visible. By this definition, there are two key words that make light a powerful event. It stimulates sight, meaning that even though there might be sight, without light stimulating that sight, it will not provide much value. The second is that it makes things visible. The existence of things does not necessarily translate into their visibility. When light comes, the invisible things are made visible, and the sight can only see them when it is stimulated by the power of light. The light does not only stimulate sight and unveil the invisible, but it also provides understanding by enlightening our minds. When the true and genuine light illuminates our lives, we comprehend the material world from the enlightened standpoint.

This light is also translated to be knowledge, wisdom, and understanding. The wise wrote in Proverbs 24, verse 3: "Through [skillful and godly] wisdom, a house [a life, a home, a family] is built, and by understanding, it is established on a sound and good foundation, and by knowledge, its roots are filled with all precious and pleasant riches." When the true light illuminates the simple, not only is their life built on a stronghold, but their stores are filled with pleasant riches—pleasant riches because their homes are filled with the peace and fulfillment that comes from the stable state of their hearts and minds.

This is the life Estelle and I built together. I was fortunate to share life with a person who had been illuminated by the light that shines in the darkness and can only be seen by those who welcome him in. "Him," because this light is a person. When he enters and we allow him to do the work, we shine brighter to impact those we encounter. Estelle has impacted my life, not because she was magically created, but rather because she truly embraced THE LIGHT. This same light continues to carry me through.

As a couple, Estelle and I had encountered the light and permitted our lives to be guided by it. I know that she had been illuminated, and I was fortunate to comprehend her value. She was my light because we shared the love that stemmed from the true light. That true light does not dim when the life it reflects through has ceased to exist. The impact remains and empowers us to continue emitting the energy endowed in our lives to illuminate those we encounter. I will continue to strive for wisdom, knowledge, and understanding that THE LIGHT can only give.

May you find THE LIGHT as you journey through your life!

Conclusion

When the gentle glow of light begins to wane, it does not signal the total obliteration of its presence, for within the fading embrace, hope persists undaunted. True fading transpires only when hope departs entirely, leaving a void of perpetual obscurity. Such a departure of hope, the cornerstone that kindles the luminance within, yields a life bereft of meaning and essence.

Journeying through the corridors of my life, particularly in the aftermath of Estelle's transition, I have unraveled the profound simplicity and intricate complexity encapsulated within life's equation, shaped by two pivotal variables: truth and dare, facts and unknown. This dichotomy, in my perception, encapsulates the entirety of our odyssey called life.

An allegory emerges in the form of the childhood game, "truth or dare," where participants stand at a crossroads of choices. To opt for truth entails laying bare unvarnished realities, regardless of gravity. Contrarily, the daring choice is an embrace of the enigmatic, an undertaking of the uncharted, and a willingness to traverse realms previously unexplored, often venturing into acts deemed implausible within ordinary confines.

This life journey mirrors these dual facets. Truth, the first variable, encapsulates the factual tapestry and realities that compose our existence. However, truths do not always align with our idealized narratives. Heartbreak, loss, injustice, unmet needs, disillusionment, and love's incongruities etch their indelible marks. These truths persist as unchangeable markers, often beyond our influence or control.

Complementing truth is the dare, the venture into the realm of the unknown. Armed with truths, stepping into the nebulous landscape becomes a daring feat. Amidst confusion and grief, it's a pledge to advance, believing in concealed illumination. Amidst heartache, it's a commitment to persevere, reaching for distant dreams. Amidst brokenness, it's a resolve to rise, piecing together fragments with tenacity, and kindling an unexpected inner light that unveils life's beauty.

This variable of daring, synonymous with hope, asserts that while truth holds sway in life's equation, it need not be the sole guiding compass. In gathering our shattered pieces, navigating hardships in their myriad intensities, there emerges a journey of purpose. By daring to advance, every incremental step lays a foundation of formidable strength, an edifice graced with the beauty born of perseverance.

Within the pages of this memoir, *When Light Fades Away, Hope Remains*, my endeavor is twofold: an acknowledgment of truth's existence interwoven in my life's fabric, coupled with the unwavering conviction that daring to persist in the face of these facts preserves a radiant, unfading ember of hope. I aspire that the vulnerable truths unveiled herein will embolden you to dare, to love, and to pursue fervently the passions almost stifled by heartaches.

Every juncture in your journey adds to the radiance you carry, dictating how your light will illuminate both your path and those you encounter. In embracing the dare, the next right step, the incandescence of your light grows exponentially, piercing the shroud of uncertainties.

Let this memoir stand as an invitation: Hope remains. Venture forth with audacious courage, dare to defy darkness, and let the brilliance of your inner light guide you through the ever-shifting mosaic of life.

Hope remains, so get out there and dare!

About the Author

Willy Gakunzi, a devoted father to his cherished daughters Kayla and Shayna, had a remarkable life journey that began in the Democratic Republic of Congo, in the high plateau of Mulenge in the South Kivu region. Raised in Rwanda, Willy now calls Toronto, Canada his home, alongside his loving family. His academic achievements include a Master of Science in International Economics and Business, from the University of Utrecht in the Netherlands. He also earned certification as a Functional Business Architect from the University of Antwerp and Cefora Institute in Belgium.

With over 15 years of expertise, Willy shines as a Banking and Financial Regulatory Risk Subject Matter expert. His proficiency lies in implementing intricate financial solutions within the banking landscape, guiding financial institutions to navigate and measure every facet of risk to calculate their risk-based capital adequacy ratio (CAR). In recognition of his exceptional leadership, Willy was honored with the **2021 CEO Award from Wolters Kluwer**. His life and professional journey have taken him across Africa, Europe, and North America, painting a global tapestry of experience.

Beyond his professional endeavors, Willy is a passionate philanthropist with a deep commitment to empowering marginalized communities through skill acquisition and access to capital. In 2019, he established the HOW Foundation (www.howfoundation.org), a vehicle through which he channels his charitable work. Music resonates as another facet of Willy's diverse talents—a singer and songwriter with an album to his name. Go to www.WhenLightFadesAwayHopeRemains.com to download his latest song, offered as a complimentary gift to readers.

The author is available for delivering keynote presentations, coaching on overcoming setbacks to maximize your potential, panel discussions, and consulting in financial services. For rates and availability, contact the author directly at: author@WhenLightFadesAwayHopeRemains.com.

To order more books, please visit: www.amazon.com.

Finally, If the pages of this book have ignited a spark within you, the greatest endeavor you can embark upon is to arise, discover the inner light, and, in turn, be an inspiring beacon for your family, community, and society. In a world yearning for hope and illumination, your radiance can shape paths and ignite hearts.